INTRODUCTION

Some of Canada's best illustrators have contributed to this Picture Dictionary, which has been carefully designed to combine words and pictures into a pleasurable learning experience.

Its unusually large number of terms (3336) makes this Picture Dictionary a flexible teaching tool. It is excellent for helping young children acquire language and dictionary skills. Because the vocabulary it encompasses is so broad, this dictionary can also be used to teach new words to older children and adults as well. Further, it is also an effective tool for teaching English as a second language.

THE VOCABULARY

The decision on which words to include and which to leave out was made in relation to three standards. First, a word-frequency analysis was carried out to include the most common words. Then a thematic clustering analysis was done to make sure that words in common themes (animals, plants, activities etc.) were included. Finally, the vocabulary was expanded to include words which children would likely hear, ask about and use. This makes this dictionary's vocabulary more honest than most. 'To choke', 'greedy', 'to smoke' are included, but approval is withheld.

This process was further complicated by the decision to *systematically* illustrate the meanings. Although the degree of abstraction was kept reasonably low, it was considered necessary to include terms such as 'to expect' and 'to forgive', which are virtually impossible to illustrate. Instead of dropping these terms, we decided to provide explanatory sentences that create a context.

Where variations occur between British and North American English, both terms are given, with an asterisk marking the British version (favor/favour*, gas/petrol*).

USING THIS DICTIONARY

Used at home, this dictionary is an enjoyable book for children to explore alone or with their parents. The pictures excite the imagination of younger children and entice them to ask questions. Older children in televisual cultures often look to visual imagery as an aid to meaning. The pictures help them make the transition from the graphic to the written. Even young adults will find the book useful, because the illustrations, while amusing, are not childish.

The dictionary as a whole provides an occasion to introduce students to basic dictionary skills. This work is compatible with school reading materials in current use, and can serve as a 'user-friendly' reference tool.

Great care has been taken to ensure that any contextual statements made are factual, have some educational value and are compatible with statements made elsewhere in the book. Lastly, from a strictly pedagogical viewpoint, the little girl featured in the book has not been made into a paragon of virtue; young users will readily identify with her imperfections.

A todos mis amigos

A lo mejor éste sea el primer diccionario de verdad que van a tener. ¡Ojalá que les guste tanto como me gusta a mí!

Yo me llamo Marisol, soy una niñita, voy a la escuela y a clases de natación. Tengo un hermanito menor y un montón de opiniones sobre un montón de cosas. Mi papá es un almirante, y si quieren conocerlo, allá se ve, en la página siguiente. El está justo en la parte de abajo. ¿Lo ven? Mi mamá aparece en la página que viene después, arriba, a la derecha. Y si quieren conocerme a mí, búsquenme en la palabra "calmada".

En este viaje que vamos a hacer juntos ustedes aprenderán muchas palabras útiles e interesantes, y algunos números también.

Cinco personas grandes se entretuvieron de lo lindo haciendo los dibujos que encontrarán en todo el libro. Uno de ellos lo hice yo (una cebra). ¿Vieron ya con qué palabra termina el diccionario?

Bueno, este libro se hizo especialmente y con mucho cariño para mis amiguitos, y yo espero que a todos les guste mucho.

PICTURE DICTIONARY

SPANISH-ENGLISH

SPANISH-ENGLISH PICTURE DICTIONARY

Illustrated by Kathryn Adams, Pat Gangnon, Colin Gillies, David Shaw and Yvonne Zan.
Designed by David Shaw and Associates.

Color separations by New Concept Limited

Typesetting by Osgoode Technical Translations

Printed in Canada by Metropole Litho Inc.

In this dictionary, as in reference works in general, no mention is made of patents, trademark rights, or other proprietary rights which may attach to certain words or entries. The absence of such mention, however, in no way implies that the words or entries in question are exempt from such rights.

English language editors: P. O'Brien-Hitching, R. LeBel, P. Rényi, K. C. Sheppard.

Spanish editors: P. Mason, L. Garcia

Originally published by Éditions Rényi Inc., Toronto, Canada

Distributed exclusively in trade and education in the United States of America by Langenscheidt Publishers, Inc., Maspeth, New York 11378

Hardcover	ISBN 0-88729-854-0
Softcover	ISBN 0-88729-860-5

Distributed outside the USA by Éditions Rényi Inc., Toronto, Canada

Hardcover	ISBN 0-921606-36-2
Softcover	ISBN 0-921606-48-6

el ábaco

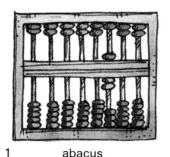

1   abacus

acerca de, a punto de

Cuéntame más **acerca de** eso.
Estoy **a punto de** partir.

Tell me about it.
I'm about to leave.

2   about

Tiene la manzana **por encima** de la cabeza.

3   above

Jorge está **ausente**.

4   absent

Todo automóvil tiene **un acelerador**.

5   accelerator

el acento

Jacques habla con **acento** francés.
Ponga **el acento** sobre la primera sílaba.

Jacques speaks with a French accent.
Put the accent on the first syllable.

6   accent

el accidente

7   accident

el acordeón

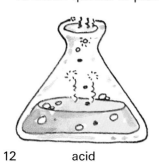

8   accordion

Todos **acusaron** a Georgina.

9   to accuse

¿Cuántos **ases** tiene la baraja?

10   ace

Me **duele** la cabeza.

11   My head aches.

El ácido quema la piel.

12   acid

De **la bellota** nace el roble.

13   acorn

la acróbata

14   acrobat

enfrente, de un extremo al otro

Jorge vive **enfrente**.
He viajado **de un extremo al otro** del país.

Jorge lives across the street.
I have travelled across the country.

15   across

Suma estas cantidades.

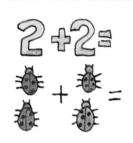

16   to add

Esta es **la dirección** de Marisol.

17   address

El papá de Marisol es **almirante.**

18   admiral

Yo te **adoro.**

19   to adore

Los adultos son personas grandes.

20   adult

avanzar

21   to advance

¿Es **una ventaja** ser alto?

22   advantage

A la mamá de Marisol le encanta **la aventura**.

23   adventure

Belisario está muy **asustado.**

24   He is afraid..

Africa es un continente.

25   Africa

después de, perseguir, tras

Puedes jugar **después de** la comida.
Ella me **persigue.**
¡Vé **tras** la pelota!

You can play after dinner.
She's after me.
Go after the ball!

26   after

La tarde empieza después del mediodía.

27   afternoon

otra vez, más

¡El partido va a empezar **otra vez!**
No lo vuelvas a hacer nunca **más.**

The game is starting again!
Don't do it ever again.

28   again

A Micifuz le gusta restregarse **contra** mis pantalones.

29   to rub against

¡Qué gran diferencia de **edades!**

30   age

Los atletas son personas muy **ágiles.**

31   agile person

un barco **encallado**

32   aground

adelante de, por adelantado

Rosita se sienta **adelante de** Martín.
Avisa tu llegada **por adelantado.**

Rosita sits ahead of Martin.
Call ahead to tell them you're coming.

33   ahead

ayudar

34   to provide aid

¿Estás **apuntando** bien?

35   to aim

La cometa se remonta por **los aires.**

36   air

el colchón inflable

37   air mattress

Hay un insecto en la campana **hermética**.

38   airtight

A este **avión** le pasa algo.

39   airplane/aeroplane*

Los aviones aterrizan en **el aeropuerto**.

40 airport

Tu butaca está junto al **pasillo**.

41 aisle

el despertador

42 alarm clock

Este es mi **álbum** de fotografías.

43 album

¡La casa está **en llamas**!

44 alight

Este está **vivo** y coleando.

45 alive

Los quiero **todos**.

46 I want them all.

Este es un gatito de **callejón**.

47 alley

el caimán

48 alligator

la almendra

49 almond

Este perrito **casi**, **casi** muerde el hueso.

50 almost

No entiendo por qué se sienta **solo**

51 alone

¡Ven **conmigo**!

52 along

en **voz alta, fuerte**

53 aloud

las letras del **alfabeto**

a b c ch d e f g h
i j k l ll m n ñ o
p q r s t u v w x y z
A B C D CH D E F G H I J
K L LL M N Ñ O P Q R S T U
V W X Y Z

54 alphabet

¿**Ya** me tengo que ir?

55 Do I have to go **already**?

Me duele un poco, pero **estoy bien**.

56 I am **alright**.

Yo **también** quiero un poco.

57 I **also** want some.

la escalera de **aluminio**

58 aluminum/aluminium* ladder

Siempre me estoy cayendo.

59 I **always** fall down.

la ambulancia	un lobo **entre** las ovejas	**el ancla**	unos restos **antiguos**
60 ambulance	61 wolf **among** sheep	62 anchor	63 ancient
el ángulo	Malandrín está **enojado**.	**los animales**	**el tobillo**
64 angle	65 He is **angry**.	66 animals	67 ankle
anunciar	**otro** sandwich	y **la respuesta** es . . .	**la hormiga**
68 to announce	69 **another** sandwich	70 The **answer** is...	71 ant
la Antártida	**el antílope**	**los cuernos, las astas, la cornamenta**	No tengo **nada** de dinero.
72 Antarctic	73 antelope	74 antlers	75 I do not have **any** money.
Las cabras se comen **cualquier cosa**.	Malandrín está enojado porque no puede salir a **ninguna parte**.	Una de las uvas está **separada** del racimo.	**el simio**
76 It eats **anything**.	77 He cannot go **anywhere**.	78 apart	79 ape

la abejera, el colmenar

80 apiary

disculparse, disculpar

Disculparse es casi lo mismo que pedir perdón. Quiero que me **disculpen** por llegar atrasado.

To apologize means to say you are sorry.
I apologize for being late!

81 to apologize/apologise*

aparecer, parecer

Apareció de la nada.
Parece que está nevando.
La Reina **apareció** en la televisión.

He appeared out of nowhere.
It appears to be snowing.
The Queen appeared on television.

82 to appear

aplaudir

83 to applaud

la manzana

84 apple

el corazón de manzana

85 apple core

acercarse, aproximarse

86 to approach

el damasco, el albaricoque

87 apricot

En abril, lluvias mil.

88 April

el delantal

89 apron

el acuario

90 aquarium

el arco

91 arch

el arquitecto

92 architect

En el Ártico hace mucho frió.

93 Arctic

discutir

94 to argue

el brazo

95 arm

el sillón

96 armchair

El Cid Campeador usaba armadura.

97 armor/armour*

la axila, el sobaco

98 armpit

dar la vuelta a, cerca de, alrededor de

La vuelta al mundo en ochenta días
A la función llegaron **cerca de** cien personas.
Toti llega a casa **alrededor del** mediodía.

Around the world in eighty days
The show attracted around one hundred people.
Toti comes home around noon.

99 around

A Jorge le gusta **arreglar** flores.	La policía **arrestó** a Malandrín.	**llegar**	**la flecha**
100 to **arrange** flowers	101 to **arrest**	102 to **arrive**	103 arrow
la alcachofa	**el artista**	**tan . . . como, en cuanto a, tal como** **Tan** pronto **como** tú quieras. **En cuanto a** ti, te has metido en un problema. **Tal como** te iba diciendo . . . *As soon as you like.* *As for you, I think you are in trouble!* *As I was saying . . .*	**la ceniza**
104 artichoke	105 artist	106 as	107 ash
el cenicero	**Asia** es un continente.	**Preguntemos** cómo llegar.	Pilar y Micifuz se quedaron **dormidos**.
108 ashtray	109 Asia	110 to **ask** for directions	111 asleep
los espárragos	Toma dos **aspirinas** para el dolor de cabeza.	Matilde **se asombra** de todo.	**el astronauta**
112 asparagus	113 aspirin	114 to **astonish**	115 astronaut
el astrónomo	**en, al, por** Rosita está **en** casa con su papá. **Al** principio no podía escuchar. **Por** lo menos me trajo flores. *Rosita is at home with her dad.* *At first I couldn't hear.* *At least he brought me flowers.*	**la atleta**	**el atlas**
116 astronomer	117 at	118 athlete	119 atlas

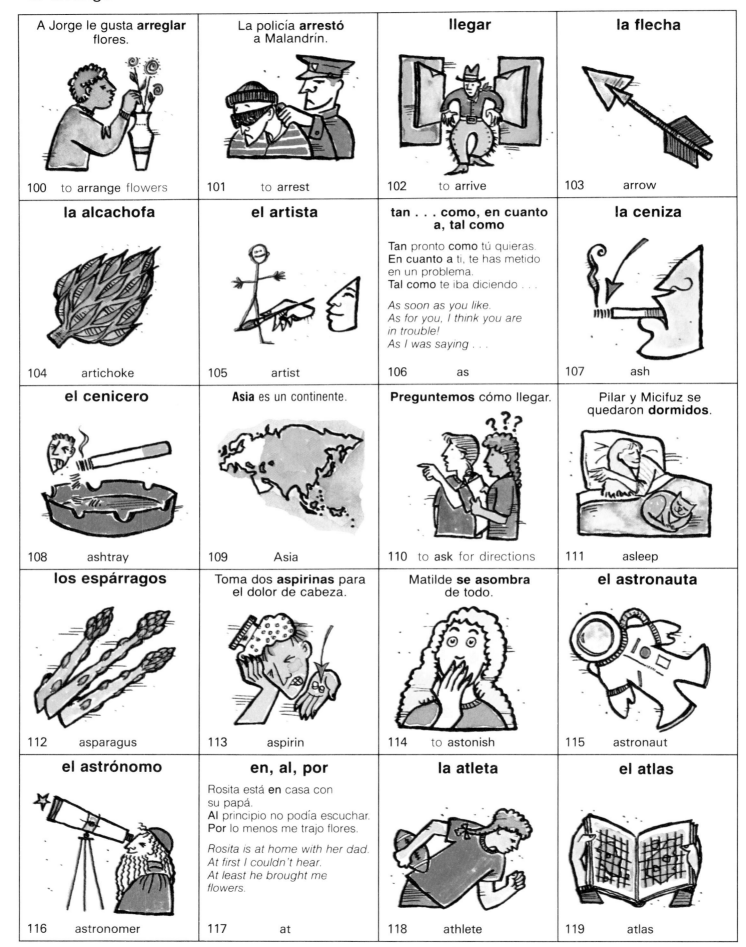

la atmósfera de la Tierra	**el átomo**	**unir, juntar**	¡Presta **atención**!
120　atmosphere	121　atom	122　to attach	123　Pay attention!
¿Qué cosas se guardan en **el desván**?	**el público**	En el hemisferio norte hace calor en **agosto**.	Mi **tía** es la hermana de mi mamá.
124　attic	125　audience	126　August	127　My aunt is my mother's sister.
Australia es una isla-continente.	**el autor, el escritor, el compositor**	un despertador **automático**	**el otoño**
128　Australia	129　author	130　automatic	131　autumn
la avalancha	**la palta, el aguacate**	¿Cómo es que todavía estás **despierto**?	Ella **no está**.
132　avalanche	133　avocado	134　awake	135　She is away.
un olor **atroz**	una persona **torpe, desgarbada**	**el hacha**	Un **eje** conecta dos ruedas.
136　an **awful** smell	137　an **awkward** person	138　axe	139　axle

B

el bebé, el nene, la criatura	**el cochecito para bebés**	Ráscame **la espalda**, por favor.
140 baby	141 baby carriage/pram*	142 back

tocino con huevos	la manzana estaba **mala**	**la insignia, el distintivo**	**retroceder**
144 bacon and eggs	145 bad apple	146 badge	143 to back up

¿Qué hay en esta **bolsa**?	El queso es el mejor **cebo** para cazar ratones.	**hornear, cocer**	**el panadero**
147 bag	148 bait	149 to bake	150 baker

la panadería	un muy buen **equilibrio**	**el balcón**	Raúl es **calvo**.
151 bakery	152 good balance	153 balcony	154 bald

la pelota, el balón	**la bailarina**	la función de **ballet**	**el globo**
155 ball	156 ballerina	157 ballet	158 balloon

el globo aerostático

159   hot air **balloon**

el plátano, la banana, el guineo

160   banana

la cinta para el pelo, el cintillo

161   band

el grupo musical

162   musical band

El doctor me puso este **vendaje**.

163   bandage

golpear, batir

164   to bang

la baranda, el pasamanos

165   banister

En **el banco** se guarda el dinero.

166   bank

la barra

167   bar

Los bares son para las personas grandes.

168   bar/pub*

la alambrada de púas

169   barbed wire

Ignacio fue al **peluquero**.

170   barber

un pie **descalzo**

171   one **bare** foot

¡A ese precio es una verdadera **ganga**!

172   bargain

la barcaza, el lanchón

173   barge

ladrar

174   to bark

La cebada crece en el campo.

176   barley

el granero

177   barn

Los soldados viven en **los cuarteles**.

178   barracks

la corteza

175   bark

el barril de aceite

179   barrel

el cañón de una pistola

180   barrel

la traba, el pasador

181   barrette/hair slide*

la barrera

182   barrier

la base de una columna

183   base

la base de béisbol

184   base

el béisbol

185   baseball

el sótano, el subterráneo

186   basement/cellar*

la albahaca

187   basil

la canasta, la cesta

188   basket

la pelota de baloncesto

189   basketball

los bates de béisbol y criquet

190   bats

Me estoy dando **un baño**.

192   I am having a bath.

la sala de baño, el cuarto de baño, el baño

193   bathroom

la tina, la bañera

194   bathtub

Los murciélagos vuelan de noche.

191   bat

Me hace falta **una pila** para mi radio.

195   battery

la bahía

196   bay

Mi mamá cocina con hojas de **laurel**.

197   bay leaves

el bazar

198   bazaar

ser, estar

Yo **soy** buen alumno.
Voy a **estar** fuera por unos días.
Marisol, ¿dónde **está** Martín?

I am a good student.
I am going to be away for a few days.
Marisol, where is Martin?

199   to be

---

la playa

200   beach

---

un collar de **cuentas**

201   bead

---

el pico de un loro

202   beak

---

el rayo, el haz de luz

203   beam of light

---

los porotos, los frijoles, las judías, las habichuelas

204   beans

Este **oso** sabe andar en bicicleta.

205   bear

Don Manuel tiene **una barba** muy larga.

206   beard

¡Qué **bestia** más horrible!

207   beast

Hilda **toca** el tambor.

208   to beat

---

una perrita **hermosa**

209   beautiful

El castor construye diques.

210   beaver

Estoy llorando **porque** . . .

211   I am crying because...

---

convertirse

212   to become

Ya es hora de irse a **la cama.**

213   bed

---

la lámpara de cabecera

214 bed lamp/reading light*

---

el dormitorio

215   bedroom

La abeja es un insecto muy útil.

216   bee

---

el haya

217   beech

Las abejas viven en **colmenas.**

218   beehive

la jarra de **cerveza**

219   beer

**la remolacha,
la betarraga**

220   beet/beetroot*

el escarabajo

221   beetle

Lávate las manos **antes
de** comer.

222 Wash your hands **before** dinner.

mendigar, pordiosear

223   to beg

**empezar, comenzar,
iniciarse**

Para **empezar**, tomemos el
desayuno.
La clase de piano de Marisol
comienza a las diez.
Las clases **se inician** en marzo.

*To begin with, let's have breakfast!
Marisol's piano lesson begins at
ten o'clock.
School begins in March.*

224   to **begin**

Eliana **se porta** muy bien.

225   to behave

Leonor está escondida
detrás del árbol.

226   behind

beige

227   beige

Yo **creo** que los dragones
sí existen.

228   I **believe** in dragons.

la campana

229   bell

el ombligo

230   belly button

Este perrito **me pertenece**
a mí.

231   He **belongs** to me.

El gato está **debajo**
de la mesa.

232   below

el cinturón

233   belt

el banco de la plaza

234   bench

el recodo en el camino

235   bend

doblar

236   to bend

la boina

237   beret

Carmen está **al lado
del** árbol.

238   beside

además de, además

¿No crees que **además del** postre deberías comer otra cosa?
Además, te hace mal tanta azúcar.

Should you not eat something else besides dessert?
Besides, you should not eat so much sugar.

239   besides

la mejor

240   best

mejor, más vale

Daniela escribe **mejor** que Esteban.
Más vale tarde que nunca.

Daniela writes better than Esteban.
Better late than never.

241   better

Felipe pasa **entre** las rocas.

242   between

el babero

243   bib

la bicicleta

244   bicycle

grande

245   big

Una **bici** es lo mismo que una bicicleta.

246   bike

el billete

247   bill/banknote*

el cartel

248   billboard/hoarding*

El billar es un juego de salón.

249   billiards/snooker*

atar, amarrar

250   to bind/tie up*

los binoculares, los prismáticos, los gemelos

251   binoculars

el pájaro, el ave

252   bird

el nacimiento

Yo soy canadiense de **nacimiento**.
¿Tú tienes un certificado de **nacimiento**?
Indica tu lugar de **nacimiento**.

I am a Canadian by birth.
Do you have a birth certificate?
State your place of birth.

253   birth

¡Feliz **cumpleaños**!

254   birthday

la galleta, el bizcocho

255   biscuit

Los dientes sirven para **morder**.

256   to bite

Saqué **un mordisco** grande.

257   bite

amargo

La cerveza tiene un sabor **amargo**.
Marisol lloró amargamente cuando se le perdió su muñeca preferida.

Beer has a bitter taste.
Marisol shed bitter tears when she lost her favorite doll.

258   bitter

negro

259　　black

la mora

260　　blackberry

el mirlo

261　　blackbird

Martín hizo un dibujo en **la pizarra.**

262　　blackboard

la grosella, el casis

263　　blackcurrant

el herrero

264　　blacksmith

la hoja de la espada

265　　blade

echar la culpa, tener la culpa

El papá le **echó la culpa** a Marisol, pero no fue ella quien lo hizo.
El que **tiene la culpa** es Luis.

Dad blamed Marisol, but she did not do it.
Luis is to blame.

266　　to blame

una hoja **en blanco**

267　　blank page

la frazada, la manta

268　　blanket

Un estallido es lo mismo que una explosión.

269　　blast

hacer volar, hacer estallar

270　　to blast

Los bomberos apagaron **el incendio.**

271　　blaze

la chaqueta, la americana

272　　blazer

El blanqueador sirve para limpiar la ropa.

273　　bleach

Me está **sangrando** la nariz.

274　　to bleed

la licuadora

275　　blender

Los ciegos no pueden ver.

276　　blind

pestañear, parpadear

277　　to blink

Las ampollas duelen mucho.

278　　blister

la tempestad de nieve

279   blizzard

¿Tú juegas con cubos?

280   block

la manzana, la cuadra

281   block

La policía le cerró el paso a Gabriel.

282   to block

la cabellera rubia

283   blond/blonde*

la transfusión de sangre

284   blood

la planta en flor

285   bloom

florecer

286   to blossom

la mancha de tinta

287   blot

la blusa

288   blouse

un golpe en la cabeza

289   a blow to the head

soplar

290   to blow

azul

291   blue

el arándano

292   blueberries

romo, brusco

Este cuchillo está **romo** y no sirve para cortar tomates.
Eliana fue muy **brusca** con él.

This knife is too blunt to cut the tomato.
Eliana was very blunt with him.

293   blunt

Isabel se ruboriza con facilidad.

294   to blush

el jabalí

295   boar

el tablero

296   board

jactarse, ufanarse

A Cristóbal le gusta **jactarse**.
De lo que más **se ufana** es de su modestia.

Cristobal likes to boast.
His modesty is nothing to boast about.

297   to boast

el bote

298   boat

la horquilla

299   bobby pin/hairgrip*

el cuerpo humano

300   body

hervir

301   to boil

el perno

302   bolt

¡A otro perro con ese **hueso**!

303   bone

la fogata, la hoguera

304   bonfire

el libro

305   book

el estante, la repisa para libros

306   bookshelf

el bumerang

307   boomerang

la bota

308   boot

Esta es **la frontera** entre dos países.

309   border

Es difícil **horadar** el cemento.

310   to bore

nacer

¿En qué año **naciste**?
Los niños **nacen** para ser felices.

What year were you born? Children are born to be happy.

312   born

pedir prestado, tomar prestado

¿Te podría **pedir prestado** algo de dinero?
A veces, Marisol **toma prestada** la bicicleta de su hermano.

Can I borrow some money? Marisol often borrows her brother's bike.

313   to borrow

el jefe

314   boss

aburrir

A veces, Marisol **aburre** a la gente.
Tomás **me aburre** porque habla demasiado.

*Sometimes, Marisol bores people.
Tomas bores me because he talks too much.*

311   to bore

los dos, ambos

Los dos vamos a ir.
Pruébate **ambos** zapatos.

*Both you and I are going.
Try on both shoes.*

315   both

la botella, el frasco

316   bottle

el abridor

317   bottle opener

el fondo

318   bottom

la roca

319   boulder

La pelota **rebotó**
en el suelo.

320   to bounce

**el ramillete,
el ramo** de flores

321   bouquet

arco y flecha

322   bow

el tazón, el bol

324   bowl

¿Qué hay dentro de
la caja?

325   box

el boxeador, el pugilista

326   boxer

**la pajarita, el corbatín, la corbata
de lazo o de humita**

323   bow tie

el niño

327   boy

el sostén

328   bra

la pulsera, el brazalete

329   bracelet

presumir, fanfarronear

María **presume** de
sus juguetes nuevos.
Su papá le dice que no hay
que **fanfarronear**.

*Maria brags about her
new toys.
Her dad tells her not to brag.*

330   to brag

el cerebro

331   brain

Todo automóvil tiene
frenos.

332   brake

frenar

333   to brake

la rama del árbol

334   branch

valiente

El dentista dice que tú eres
muy **valiente**.

*The dentist says you are
very brave.*

335   brave

el pan

336   bread

romper, quebrar

337   to break

**descomponerse, echarse
a perder, fallar**

338   to break down

Un ladrón **entró a robar**.	**el desayuno**	mal **aliento**	**respirar**
339 to break in	340 breakfast	341 breath	342 to breathe
Mi casa está hecha de **ladrillos**.	Gabriela trabaja como **albañil**.	**La novia** es tímida.	Y **el novio** también.
343 brick	344 bricklayer	345 bride	346 bridegroom
el puente	Los caballos llevan **bridas**.	**el maletín, la cartera, el portafolio**	El sol está muy **brillante**.
347 bridge	348 bridle	349 briefcase	350 bright sun
Macabeo me **trae** las zapatillas.	Marisol viene a **devolver** libros a la biblioteca.	vidrio **quebradizo**	**el brécol, el bróculi, el brócoli**
351 to bring	352 to bring back	353 brittle glass	354 broccoli
el broche, el prendedor	**Un arroyo** es un río pequeño.	**la escoba**	Yo quiero mucho a mi **hermano**.
355 brooch	356 brook	357 broom	358 I love my brother.

las cejas, la frente

359   brow

marrón, café

360   brown

A Daniel le hace falta **cepillarse** el pelo.

362   to brush

el cepillo, la escobilla

363   brush

la herida, el golpe, la magulladura

361   bruise

los repollitos, la col de Bruselas

366   brussels sprouts

la brocha, el pincel

364   paintbrush

el cepillo de dientes

365   toothbrush

la burbuja

367   bubble

el cubo, el balde, la cubeta

368   bucket

la hebilla

369   belt buckle

el capullo, el botón, el brote, el cogollo

370   bud

el búfalo, el bisonte

371   buffalo

el bicho, la sabandija

372   bug

la corneta, el clarín

373   bugle

construir, edificar

374   to build

el toro

375   bull

la excavadora, la niveladora, el buldozer

376   bulldozer

Las balas son muy peligrosas.

377   bullet

el megáfono, el altoparlante

378 bullhorn/megaphone*

Javier es **un matón**.	**el chichón**	**los parachoques**	**el manojo** de espárragos
379 bully	380 bump	381 bumpers	382 bunch
el atado	**la boya, la baliza**	**el ladrón**	El fuego **ardió** con rapidez.
383 bundle	384 buoy	385 burglar	386 to burn
El globo **se reventó**.	**enterrar, sepultar**	**el autobús, el bus, el ómnibus**	**la parada de autobús, el paradero**
387 to burst	388 to bury	389 bus	390 bus stop
Un arbusto es más pequeño que un árbol.	Ahora estoy **ocupado**.	**pero, sino** Me gustaría ir, **pero** estoy ocupado. Hoy no es lunes, **sino** martes. *I would like to go, but I am busy.* *Today is not Monday, but Tuesday.*	**el carnicero**
391 bush	392 I am **busy** now.	393 but	394 butcher
¿Quieres pan con **mantequilla**?	**la mariposa**	tres **botones**	Felipe **compra** un helado.
395 butter	396 butterfly	397 buttons	398 to buy

C

el repollo, la col

399   cabbage

una cabaña en el bosque

400   cabin

la cómoda, el armario

401   cabinet

el cable

402   cable/lead*

el cacto, el cactus

403   cactus

la jaula

404   cage

el pastel, la torta

405   cake

el calculador, la calculadora

406   calculator

el calendario, el almanaque

407   calendar

el ternero, el becerro

408   calf

llamar

409   to call

Marisol se ve siempre muy **calmada.**

412   She is **calm.**

el camello

413   camel

la cámara, la máquina fotográfica

414   camera

suspender, cancelar

Si llueve vamos a **suspender** el paseo.
Marisol **canceló** la visita al zoológico.

We will call off the picnic if it rains.
Marisol has called off our trip to the zoo.

410   to **call** off

Mi papá y yo salimos a **acampar.**

415   to camp

el campamento

416   campsite

la lata, el bote, el tarro

417   can

llamar por teléfono, telefonear

411   to **call** up/to phone*

el abrelatas

418 can opener/tin* opener

Los barcos pasan por **el canal**.

419 canal

el canario

420 canary

la vela

421 candle

la palmatoria

422 candlestick

los caramelos

423 candy/sweets*

El bastón sirve de apoyo al caminar.

424 cane/walking stick*

el cañón

425 cannon

No puedo ver nada.

426 I cannot see.

la canoa

427 canoe

el melón

428 cantaloupe

El río corre por el fondo del **cañón**.

429 canyon

la gorra, el gorro

430 cap

¿Dónde queda **el Cabo de Hornos**?

431 cape

aventuras de **capa** y espada

432 cape

una letra **mayúscula**

N

433 capital

Este es **el capitán** del barco.

434 captain

capturar, atrapar

435 to capture

el automóvil, el coche, el carro

436 car

La caravana cruza el desierto.

437 caravan

los naipes, las cartas	**el cartón**	Las enfermeras **cuidan** a los enfermos.	Este es un niño **descuidado**.
438 cards	439 cardboard	440 to care	441 He is careless.
la carga	**los claveles**	**Un carnaval** es una fiesta muy grande.	**la carpintera**
442 cargo	443 carnation	444 carnival	445 carpenter
la alfombra, el tapiz, el tapete	**el carrito, el cochecito**	**la zanahoria**	El Sr. Martínez **lleva** una carga muy pesada.
446 carpet	447 carriage/pram*	448 carrot	449 to carry
el carretón, la carreta	**la caja de cartón**	**trinchar**	**la caja**
450 cart	451 carton	452 to carve	453 case
Tener **plata** es lo mismo que tener dinero.	**las castañas de cajú, las nueces de acajú**	**el castillo**	**el gato**
454 cash	455 cashew nuts	456 castle	457 cat

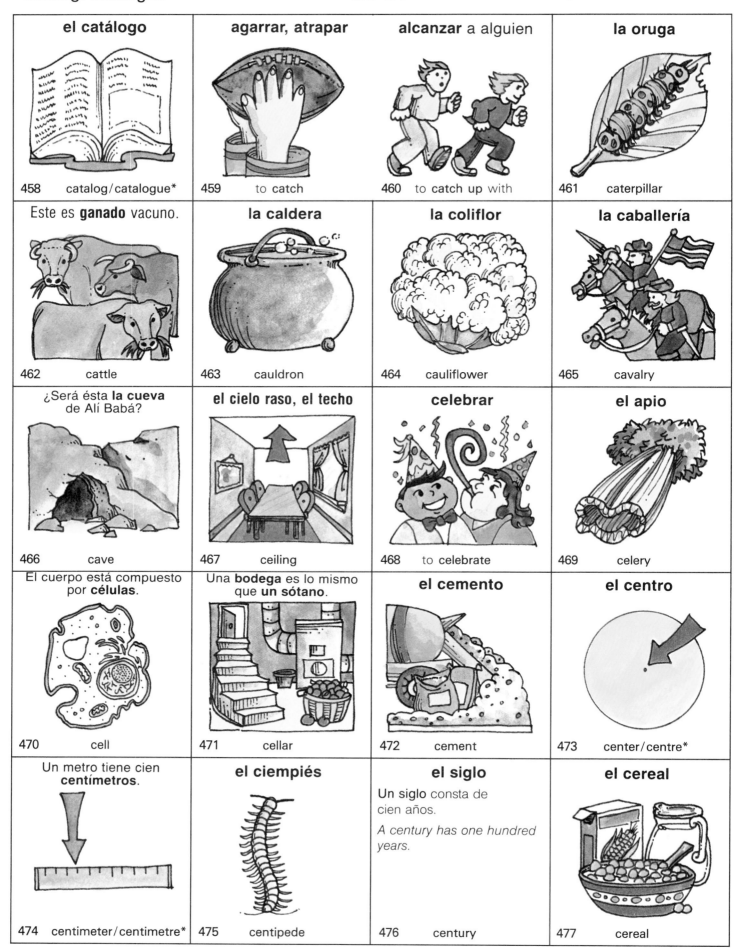

el catálogo

458   catalog/catalogue*

agarrar, atrapar

459   to catch

alcanzar a alguien

460   to catch up with

la oruga

461   caterpillar

Este es **ganado** vacuno.

462   cattle

la caldera

463   cauldron

la coliflor

464   cauliflower

la caballería

465   cavalry

¿Será ésta **la cueva** de Alí Babá?

466   cave

el cielo raso, el techo

467   ceiling

celebrar

468   to celebrate

el apio

469   celery

El cuerpo está compuesto por **células**.

470   cell

Una **bodega** es lo mismo que **un sótano**.

471   cellar

el cemento

472   cement

el centro

473   center/centre*

Un metro tiene cien **centímetros**.

474   centimeter/centimetre*

el ciempiés

475   centipede

el siglo

Un siglo consta de cien años.

A century has one hundred years.

476   century

el cereal

477   cereal

seguro, cierto

Marisol está **segura** de tener la razón.
Marcelo le causó **cierta** impresión.

Marisol is certain that she is right.
She has a certain feeling about Marcelo.

478   certain

el certificado

479   certificate

la cadena

480   chain

la sierra de cadena, la motosierra

481   chainsaw

la silla

482   chair

la tiza

483   chalk

la campeona

484   champion

el cambio, el vuelto, el sencillo

485   change

el canal

487   channel

Este libro tiene varios **capítulos**.

488   chapter

el carácter, el personaje

Marisol tiene **un carácter** muy fuerte.
Ella es todo **un personaje**.
¿Qué quiere decir este **carácter**?

Marisol has a strong character.
She is quite a character.
What does this character mean?

489   character

Raúl **se cambió** de ropa.

486   to change

el carbón

490   charcoal

la acelga

491   chard

formular cargos, cargar

La policía **formuló cargos** de robo en contra de Malandrín.
Tu juguete dejó de funcionar porque se me olvidó **cargarle** las pilas.

The police charged Malandrin with robbery.
Your toy has stopped because I forgot to charge the battery.

492   to charge

la cuadriga

493   chariot

el gráfico

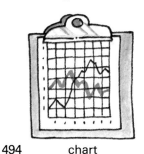

494   chart

perseguir

495   to chase

charlar

496   to chat

un lápiz **barato** y una corona **cara**

497   **cheap** pencil, expensive crown

498   to cheat

César está tratando de **hacer trampa.**

499   to check

revisar, dejar

¿**Revisaste** tus tareas antes de entregarlas?
Deje el abrigo a la entrada, por favor.

Did you check your homework before handing it in?
Check your coat at the entrance, please.

500   cheek

la mejilla

501   cheese

El queso se hace a partir de la leche.

502   cheque*/check

el cheque

503   cherries

las cerezas, las guindas

504   chest

a lo hecho, **pecho**

505   chestnut

la castaña

506   to chew

Mastica bien antes de tragar.

507   chick peas

los garbanzos

508   chicken

el pollo, la polla

509   chicken-pox

la varicela

510   chief

el comandante en **jefe**

511   child

la niña

512   a chilly day

un día **helado**

513   chimney

la chimenea

514   chimpanzee

el chimpancé

515   chin

el mentón, la barbilla

516   china/crockery*

la vajilla de porcelana

517   chip

de tal palo, tal **astilla**

El escultor talla con **un cincel**.	**las cebolletas, los cebollines**	la barra de **chocolate**	¿Te gusta cantar a **coro**?
518 chisel	519 chives	520 chocolate	521 choir
Ahogar a alguien es pésima broma.	Pedro **se atoró** con un hueso de pollo.	Quisiera **escoger** uno de éstos.	**Picar** cebollas hace llorar.
522 to choke	523 to choke on	524 to choose	525 to chop
los palillos chinos	**el cromado** del parachoques	**el crisantemo**	**el trozo** de carbón
526 chopsticks	527 chrome	528 chrysanthemum	529 a chunk/lump* of coal
Los puros son hediondos.	**Los cigarrillos** hacen muy mal.	**el círculo**	**el circo**
530 cigar	531 cigarette	532 circle	533 circus
Yo vivo en **una ciudad**.	**Las almejas** viven en su concha.	tablas sujetas con **grapa**	**aplaudir, batir palmas**
534 city	535 clam	536 clamp	537 to clap

la sala de clases, el aula

538   classroom

Los cangrejos tienen unas **pinzas** grandes.

539   claw

la arcilla, la greda

La arcilla se usa para hacer ladrillos.
Con la greda se pueden hacer ollas y platos.

Clay is used to make bricks.
You can also make pots and dishes out of clay.

540   clay

Ella está **limpia**, él está sucio.

541   She is all **clean.**

La tía Julia **levanta** la mesa.

542   to clear

el acantilado

543   cliff

Vamos **escalando** hacia la cumbre.

544   to climb

la clínica

545   clinic

recortar

546   to clip

el reloj

547   clock

cerrar

548   to close

el armario, el ropero

549   closet/cupboard*

la tela, el mantel, el paño

Las ropas se hacen con **tela**.
Hay **un mantel** en la mesa.
Mi mamá usa **un paño** de cocina para secar los platos.

Clothes are made out of cloth.
There is a tablecloth on the table.
Mother uses a dishcloth to wipe the dishes.

550   cloth

la ropa

551   clothes

el tendedero

552   clothes line

la nube

553   cloud

Los tréboles de cuatro hojas traen suerte.

554   clover

el payaso

555   clown

Cataplúm sale a cazar armado de **una maza**.

556   club

la pista, el indicio

La policía encontró **una pista** para resolver el delito.
Yo te voy a dar **un indicio**.

The police found a clue to the crime.
I will give you a clue.

557   clue

Los coches automáticos no tienen pedal de **embrague**.

558   clutch

¡**Agárrate** bien!

559   to clutch

Este es mi **entrenador**.

560   coach

Vamos viajando en **un bus** interprovincial.

561   coach

El carbón sale de las minas.

563   coal

tosco, grosero

Esta tela es muy **tosca**.
El es un tipo muy **grosero**.

This cloth is very coarse.
He is a very coarse man.

564   coarse

la costa, el litoral

565   coast

entrenar

Isabel **entrena** al equipo dos veces por semana.

Isabel coaches the team twice a week.

562   to coach

En invierno hace falta **un** buen **abrigo**.

566   coat

La casa de la araña se llama **telaraña**.

567   cobweb

el cacao

568   cocoa

el coco

569   coconut

el bacalao

570   cod

El **cafeto** es el árbol del **café**.

571   coffee

el ataúd

572   coffin

la espiral, el serpentín

573   coil

una moneda

574   coin

Tengo **frío**.

575   I am cold.

el cuello de la camisa

576   collar

La hermana de Lucía **colecciona** estampillas.

577   to collect

La universidad es una escuela para grandes.

578   college

Los coches **chocan** si se duermen los conductores.

579   to collide

un choque de automóviles

580   collision

¿Cuál es tu **color** preferido?

581   color/colours*

la yegua con su **potrillo**

582   colt

columnas de mármol

583   column

el peine, la peineta

584   comb

peinar

585   to comb

Combina bien los ingredientes.

586   combine

venir

Dile a Juan que **venga** a casa.
Marisol **vino** a la fiesta en autobús.
¿Tú **vienes** siempre por aquí?
¡**Vamos**, cuéntame!

Tell Juan to come home.
Marisol came to the party by bus.
Do you come here often?
Come on, tell me!

587   to come

Se me **soltó** en la mano.

588   to come off

Tuvo un desmayo, pero ya **volvió en sí.**

589   to come to

cómodo, confortable

590   comfortable

Una coma de verdad es mucho más pequeña.

591   comma

ordenar, mandar

592   to command

la comunidad, comunitario

Nosotros vivimos en **una comunidad** pequeña.
En el centro **comunitario** hay una piscina.
La construcción de la escuela fue un esfuerzo **comunitario**.

We live in a small community.
There is a pool at the community center.
Building the school was a community effort.

593   community

Martín y Daniel son **compañeros**.

594   companion

Estoy en buena **compañía**.

595   I am in good **company**.

comparar

596   to compare

Mi **brújula** apunta al norte.

597   My **compass** points north.

Ludwig **compone** una sinfonía.

598   to compose

el compositor

599   composer

una composición para piano

600   composition

el computador, la computadora, el ordenador

601   computer

concentrarse

602   to concentrate

el concierto

603   concert

el concreto

604   concrete

el director de la orquesta

605   conductor

el cono

607   cone

el helado de **barquillo**

608   ice cream cone

El fruto del pino se llama **piña**.

609   pine cone

el conductor

606   conductor/guard*

confiado

610   confident

Estoy **confundido**.

611   I am confused

felicitar, congratular

612   to congratulate

conectar

613   to connect

la consonante

Las letras b, c, d, f, g son **consonantes**.

B, c, d, f, g are consonants.

614   consonant

Si te pierdes, pregúntale a **un policía**.

615   constable

Una constelación tiene muchas estrellas.

616   constellation

En el mundo hay siete **continentes**.

617   continent

una animada **conversación**	Mi papá es buen **cocinero**.	El **prepara** el desayuno.	¡No le robes **las galletas** a mamá!
618 conversation	619 Dad is a good **cook**.	620 He **cooks** breakfast.	621 cookie/biscuit*
Tengo la mano en agua **fría**.	la cañería de **cobre**	**copiar**	Este pececillo vive en un arrecife de **coral**.
622 My hand is in the **cool** water.	623 copper	624 to copy	625 coral
la cuerda, el cordel	**el corcho**	**el sacacorchos, el tirabuzón**	A Marisol le encanta comer **maíz**.
626 cord	627 cork	628 corkscrew	629 corn/maize*
el rincón	**el cadáver**	**el pasillo, el corredor**	**el cosmonauta**
630 corner	631 corpse	632 corridor	633 cosmonaut/astronaut*
un traje del siglo pasado	**la cabaña**	la camisa de **algodón**	**el sofá, el sillón**
634 costume	635 cottage	636 cotton	637 couch/sofa*

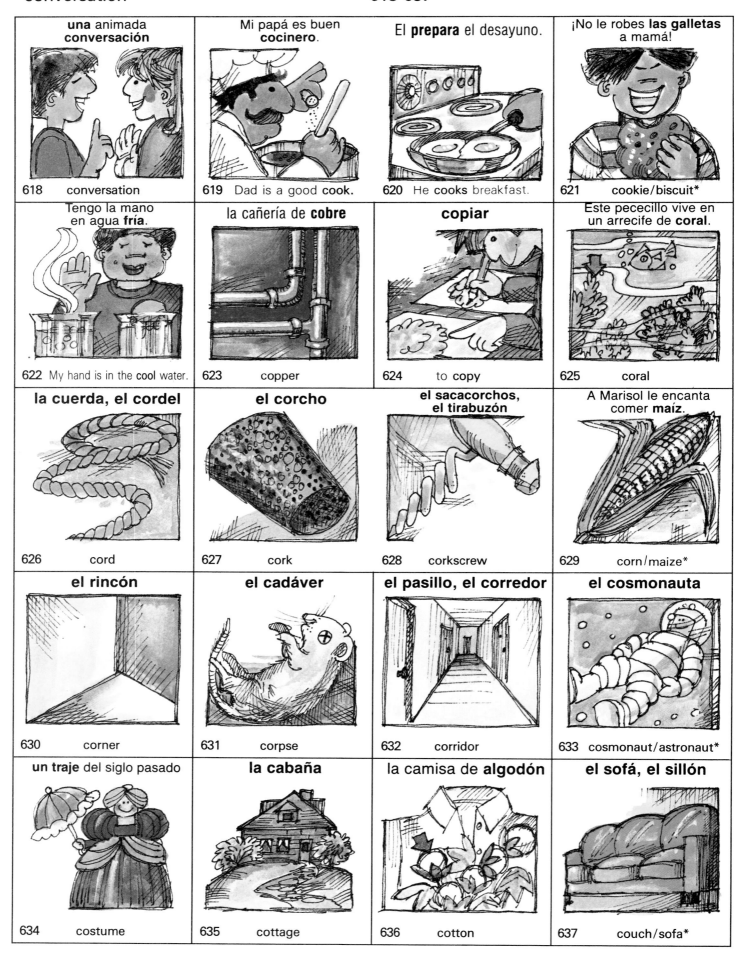

Manuela **tose** con discreción.

638　to cough

contar

639　to count

el contador

640　counter

¡Ponlo en **el mostrador**!

641　counter

¿Te gusta ir al **campo**?

642　country

Este **país** se llama Canadá.

643　country

Mi papá y mi mamá forman **una pareja**.

644　couple

Para pelear con dragones hace falta mucho **valor**.

645　courage

la cancha, **la pista** de tenis

646　court

Mi **prima** es la hija de mi tío.

647　My cousin is my uncle's daughter.

cubrir, tapar

648　to cover

Esta olla tiene **una tapa**.

649　cover

la vaca

650　cow

Este niño es un poco **cobarde**.

651　This boy is a coward.

el vaquero

652　cowboy

Las jaibas viven en el mar.

653　crab

Este florero tiene **una grieta**.

654　crack

la galleta salada

655　cracker

la cuna

656　cradle

la garza, la grulla

657　crane

la grúa

658   crane

estrellarse, chocar

659   to crash

¿Qué hay dentro de **la caja**?

660   crate

gatear

661   to crawl

el langostino

662   crayfish

los lápices de cera

663   crayons

la crema

A papá le gusta el café con **crema**.
Me gustan los duraznos con **crema**.
La crema para el sol te proteje la piel.

Dad likes cream in his coffee.
I like peaches and cream.
Sun cream protects your skin.

664   cream

la raya, el pliegue, el doblez

665   crease

¡Qué **bicho** más raro!

666   creature

Un riachuelo es un río pequeño.

667   creek

la tripulación

668   the crew

la cuna

669   crib/cot*

el grillo

670   cricket

el criminal

671   criminal

el cocodrilo

672   crocodile

Los azafranes brotan en primavera.

673   crocus

¡Esa **bribona** robó una manzana!

674   crook

un palo **torcido**

675   crooked post

El cuadro está **torcido**, pero la torre está derecha.

676 crooked painting, upright tower

una buena **cosecha**

677   crop

la cruz	Mira bien antes de **cruzar**.	**tachar, tarjar**	**el cuervo**
678 cross	679 to cross	680 to cross out	681 crow

un gentío muy grande en un espacio muy pequeño	**la corona**	Don Alfonso **corona** a la reina.	**las migajas**
682 A big **crowd** in a small space.	683 crown	684 to crown	685 crumb

Para hacer vino hay que **triturar** las uvas.	A Lucía le encanta **la corteza**.	**la muleta**	**llorar**
686 to crush	687 crust	688 crutch	689 to cry

la bola de **cristal**	**Un osezno** es un oso pequeño.	**el cubo**	**el cuclillo**
690 crystal	691 cub	692 cube	693 cuckoo

el pepino	**el puño** de la camisa	**la taza** de té	En **el aparador** hay un jarro.
694 cucumber	695 cuff	696 cup	697 cupboard

el borde de la acera, la cuneta

698   curb/kerb*

curarse, sanar

699   I am cured.

Adriana **se encrespó** el pelo.

700   to curl

Y ahora tiene el pelo **rizado**.

701   curly

Georgina es muy **curiosa**.

702   curious

las grosellas

703   currant

la corriente del río

704   current

las cortinas

705   curtains

la curva

706   curve

el cojín

707   cushion

el cliente

708   customer

cortar

709   to cut

linda, mona, graciosa

712   cute/sweet*

la cuchillería, los cubiertos

713   cutlery

la bicicleta

714   cycle

ponerse por delante, interponerse

710   to cut in

el cilindro

715   cylinder

los platillos

716   cymbals

el ciprés

717   cypress

¿Te gusta recortar?

711   to cut out

El narciso es una flor de primavera.

718   daffodil

el puñal

719   dagger

el diario, el periódico

720   daily

De las vacas obtenemos **productos lácteos**.

721   dairy

la margarita

722   daisy

Las represas están hechas de cemento.

723   dam

dañado, estropeado

724   damaged

húmedo

725   damp

bailar

726   to dance

la bailarina

727   dancer

El diente de león es una maleza.

728   dandelion

peligro

729   danger

¡Aquí está **oscuro**!

730   dark

¿Te gusta el juego de **los dardos**?

731   dart

el tablero de instrumentos

732   dashboard

¿Qué **fecha** es hoy?

733   date

Mi **hija** se llama Cristina.

734   daughter

Este va a ser un hermoso **día**.

735   the start of a nice **day**

un ratón **muerto**

736   **dead** mouse

No hay peor **sordo** que el que no quiere oír.

737 deaf

querido

Luis es un amigo muy **querido**.
¡**Querida m**amá, lo estoy pasando muy bien!
Mi hermano me es muy **querido**.

Luis is my dear friend.
Dear Mom, I'm having a great time!
My brother is very dear to me.

738 dear

Diciembre es el último mes del año.

739 December

decidir, decidirse

Marisol no logra **decidir** qué vestido ponerse.
Su mamá dice que tendrá que **decidirse** ahora mismo.

Marisol cannot decide what to wear.
Mom says she'll have to decide now.

740 to decide

la cubierta de un barco

741 deck

Este es el pirata Coqui **adornando** un arbolito.

742 to decorate

el adorno de Navidad

743 decoration

Rodrigo prefiere no nadar en la parte **profunda**.

744 deep end

Los venados viven en el bosque.

745 deer

entregar, repartir

746 to deliver

Martín me **abolló** el auto.

747 to dent

la dentista

748 dentist

las grandes tiendas, los grandes almacenes

749 department store

el desierto

750 desert

¿Qué hace **un escritorio** en el desierto?

751 desk

el postre

752 dessert

Godzilla **destruyó** toda la ciudad.

753 to destroy

Un destructor es un buque de guerra.

754 destroyer

un famoso **detective**

755 detective

Por la mañana hay **rocío** en las hojas.

756 dew

una línea **diagonal**

757   diagonal

el diagrama

758   diagram

el diamante

759   diamond

Los bebés necesitan **pañales**.

760   diaper/nappy*

Viviana lleva **un diario** de vida.

761   diary

Búscalo en **el diccionario**.

762   dictionary

morir, morirse

763   to die

la diferencia

Todas las personas nacen iguales; no hay ninguna **diferencia** entre ellas.
Hay mucha **diferencia** entre el día y la noche.

All people are born equal, there is no difference between them. There is quite a difference between night and day.

764   difference

gentes **diferentes** . . . pero iguales

765   different people

cavar

766   to dig

La serpiente **digiere** un elefante.

767   The snake **digests** an elephant.

en **penumbras**

768   dim

A Lucía se le forman **hoyuelos** en las mejillas.

769   dimple

el bote de goma

770   dinghy

el comedor

771   dining room

la comida, la cena

772   dinner

el dinosaurio

773   dinosaur

la dirección, el rumbo

774   direction

Mi papá pisó donde había **mugre** . . .

775   dirt

. . . y se le pusieron los pantalones **sucios**.

776   dirty

Estoy en total **desacuerdo** contigo.

777   to disagree

La manzana de abajo **desapareció**.

778   to disappear

el desastre

779   disaster

descubrir

780   to discover

discutir

781   to discuss

la peste

782   disease

A Marisol le encantan **los disfraces.**

783   disguise

¡Marisol, ven a lavar **los platos**, por favor!

784   dishes

un tipo **deshonesto**

785   a dishonest person

agua de lavar los platos, **lavazas**

786   dishwater

¡No me gusta esta comida!

787   to dislike

La tableta **se disuelve** en el agua.

788   to dissolve

El espacio entre dos cosas se llama **distancia**.

789   distance between two trees

Decir **distante** es decir que está lejos.

790   a distant tree

Yo vivo en este **distrito.**

791   district

Estamos cavando **una zanja**.

792   ditch

zambullirse

793   to dive

Dividimos la manzana en dos.

794   to divide

Me siento **mareado**.

795   I feel dizzy.

¿Qué debo **hacer**?

796   What shall I do?

el muelle, el atracadero  797 dock	**el doctor** 798 doctor	¿Será éste **el perro** del hortelano? 799 dog	**la muñeca** 800 doll
el delfín 801 dolphin	**la cúpula** 802 dome	**El burro** de San Vicente lleva carga y no la siente. 803 donkey	**la puerta** 804 door
el tirador, el pomo, la perilla 805 doorknob	¿Ves **doble**? 806 double	Con **la masa** se hace el pan. 807 dough	**La paloma** es el símbolo de la paz. 808 dove
Marisol tiene una almohada de **plumón**. 809 down	**dormitar** 810 to doze	**Una docena** quiere decir doce. 811 dozen	¡No lo **arrastres** por el suelo! 812 to drag
el dragón 813 dragon	**la libélula** 814 dragonfly	**el desagüe** 815 drain/plug hole*	Martín **dibuja** muy bien. 816 to draw

¡Levanten **el puente levadizo**!

817 drawbridge

Marisol guarda su ropa en este **cajón**.

818 drawer

un hermoso **sueño**

819 a nice **dream**

Toti **sueña** con ovejitas.

820 I **dream** of sheep.

el vestido

821 dress

vestirse

822 to **dress**

El **cajón** de la ropa de Marisol es parte de esta **cómoda**.

823 dresser/chest of drawers*

babear

824 to **dribble**

Quedar a la deriva no tiene ninguna gracia.

825 to **drift**

Gabriela **taladra** sobre la madera.

826 to **drill**

el taladro eléctrico

827 drill

el trago

828 drink

gotear

830 to **drip**

Yo **manejo** con mucho cuidado.

831 I **drive** carefully.

El conductor imprudente siempre termina mal.

832 crazy **driver**

tomar, beber

829 to **drink**

la llovizna

Hay una ligera **llovizna**.

There is a light drizzle.

833 drizzle

babear

834 to **drool**

No quedó ni **una gota**.

835 drop

Se me **cayó** la copa.

836 to **drop**

¡Te **vine a ver** de paso!

837   to drop in

Papá **pasó a dejar** el gato al veterinario.

838   Dad drops off the cat at the vet.

abandonar, salirse

839   to drop out

Me siento muy **amodorrado**.

840   I feel drowsy.

el tambor

841   drum

seco

842   dry

secar

843   to dry

limpiado **en seco**

844   dry cleaner

Pon la ropa mojada en **la secadora**.

845   dryer

la duquesa

846   duchess

el pato

847   duck

Batirse a **duelo** no soluciona nada.

848   duel

el duque

849   duke

el basural, el vertedero, el basurero

850   dump

botar, descargar

851   to dump

el camión de volteo, el camión tolva

852   dumptruck/lorry*

El ladrón lleva años en **el calabozo**.

853   dungeon

el crepúsculo

854   dusk

el polvo

855   dust

el enano

856   dwarf

E

Cada uno tiene una zanahoria.

857 **Each** rabbit has a carrot.

Las águilas son aves en peligro de extinción.

858 eagle

el oído, la oreja

859 ear

No por mucho madrugar amanece más **temprano**.

860 early

ganar, ganarse

Mi mamá **gana** un buen sueldo.
Marisol se ha **ganado** unas vacaciones.
El dinero tienes que **ganártelo** antes de poder gastarlo.

Mom earns a good wage.
Marisol has earned a holiday.
You must earn it before you spend it.

861 to **earn**

el planeta **Tierra**

862 Earth

la palada de **tierra**

863 earth

el terremoto

864 earthquake

el caballete, el atril

865 easel

El este es lo mismo que el oriente.

866 east

Aprender a nadar es muy **fácil**.

867 Swimming is **easy**.

comer

868 to eat

tomar el desayuno

869 to eat breakfast

almorzar

870 to eat lunch

comer, cenar

871 to eat dinner/supper*

¿Oyes **el eco** . . . eco . . . eco . . .?

872 echo

el eclipse de sol

873 eclipse

El árbol está al **borde** del barranco

874 The tree is at the **edge**.

la anguila

875 eel

La gallina francolina puso **un huevo** en la cocina.	**la berenjena**	**ocho**	**octavo**
876　　egg	877　　eggplant/aubergine*	878　　eight	879　　eighth
el elástico	**el codo**	**la elección** Los gobiernos se eligen por medio de **las elecciones**. ¿Quién ganó **las elecciones**? Esta **elección** fue muy reñida. *Elections are held to choose the government.* *Who won the election?* *The election was very close.*	**el electricista**
880　　elastic	881　　elbow	882　　election	883　　electrician
la electricidad	**el elefante**	**el ascensor**	**el ante**
884　　electricity	885　　elephant	886　　elevator/lift*	887　　elk
el olmo	Mario me **dejó en vergüenza.**	**abrazar, abrazarse**	**el bordado**
888　　elm	889　　to embarrass	890　　to embrace	891　　embroidery
la emergencia	Este frasco está **vacío.**	Este es **el fin** del camino.	Ojalá que algún día dejen de ser **enemigos.**
892　　emergency	893　　The jar is empty.	894　　This is the end.	895　　enemies

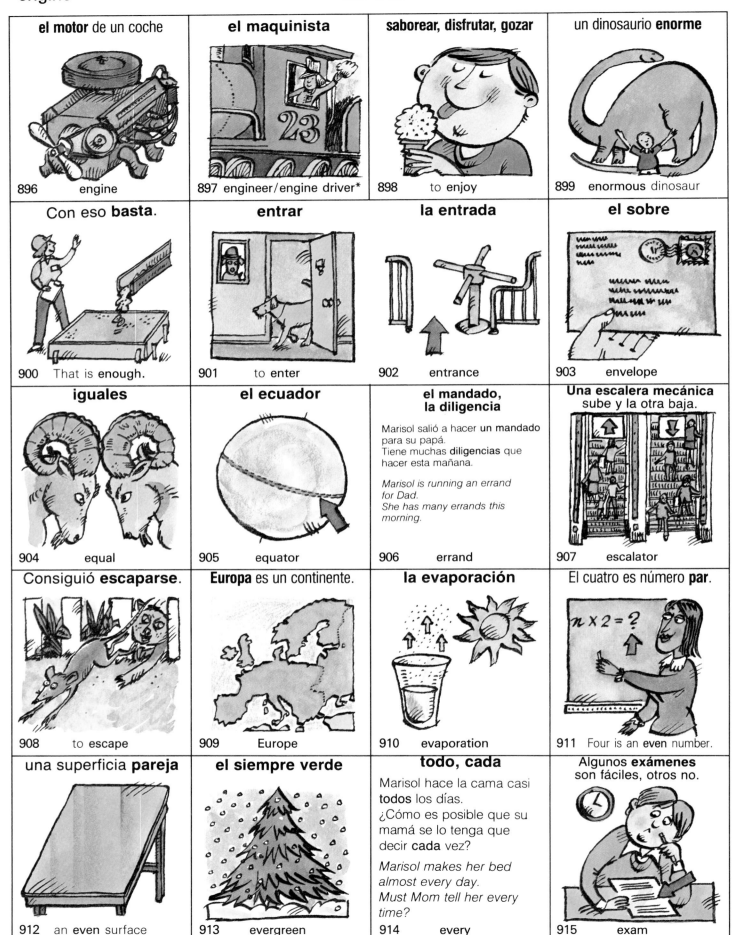

el motor de un coche
896   engine

el maquinista
897   engineer/engine driver*

saborear, disfrutar, gozar
898   to enjoy

un dinosaurio **enorme**
899   enormous dinosaur

Con eso **basta**.
900   That is **enough**.

entrar
901   to enter

la entrada
902   entrance

el sobre
903   envelope

iguales
904   equal

el ecuador
905   equator

el mandado, la diligencia

Marisol salió a hacer **un mandado** para su papá.
Tiene muchas **diligencias** que hacer esta mañana.

Marisol is running an errand for Dad.
She has many errands this morning.

906   errand

Una escalera mecánica sube y la otra baja.
907   escalator

Consiguió **escaparse**.
908   to escape

Europa es un continente.
909   Europe

la evaporación
910   evaporation

El cuatro es número **par**.
911   Four is an **even** number.

una superficia **pareja**
912   an **even** surface

el siempre verde
913   evergreen

todo, cada

Marisol hace la cama casi **todos** los días.
¿Cómo es posible que su mamá se lo tenga que decir **cada** vez?

Marisol makes her bed almost every day.
Must Mom tell her every time?

914   every

Algunos **exámenes** son fáciles, otros no.
915   exam

examinar

916   to examine

el ejemplo

A veces Marisol no da muy buen ejemplo.
Las cosas se entienden más fácilmente cuando se pone un ejemplo.

Sometimes Marisol does not set a good example.
Things are easier to understand when you give an example.

917   example

el signo de exclamación

918   exclamation mark

¡Disculpe!

919   Excuse me!

María Paz hace ejercicios todos los días.

920   to exercise

existir

Existir es lo mismo que ser.
Marisol dice "no hay tal cosa" cuando quiere decir "eso no existe".

To exist is to be.
Marisol said "There is no such thing", and she meant "It does not exist".

921   to exist

salir

922   to exit/leave*

Este globo se va a expandir hasta reventarse.

923   to expand

---

esperar, contar con

Te esperamos a las dos de la tarde.
Papá cuenta con que te portes bien.
Anita no puede esperar otra cosa.

We expect you at two o'clock.
Dad expects you to be good.
Anita cannot expect any more.

924   to expect

caro

925   expensive

el experimento

926   experiment

la experta

927   expert

Déjame explicarte lo que pasa.

928   to explain

explorar

929   to explore

la explosión

930   explosion

el extintor de incendios

931   extinguisher

---

el ojo

932   eye

la ceja

933   eyebrow

los anteojos, los lentes, las gafas

934   eyeglasses/spectacles*

la pestaña

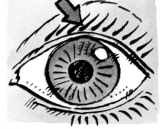

935   eyelash

936 fable — ¿Conoces **la fábula** de la hormiga y el saltamontes?

937 face — la cara, el rostro

938 factory — la fábrica

939 to fail — Juan **reprobó** el examen.

940 to fail — **fallar, averiarse**

941 fair — la feria

942 fairy — ¿Te gustan los cuentos de **hadas**?

943 faith — la fe

Tenemos mucha **fe** en ti. Marisol aceptó de buena **fe**.

We have faith in you. Marisol accepted it in good faith.

944 fake painting — Este cuadro es **falso**.

945 fall/autumn* — En **el otoño** se caen las hojas.

946 to fall — caer, caerse

949 false alarm — ¡Una **falsa** alarma! Era un asado a la parrilla.

950 family — la familia

947 to fall down — caer, caerse al suelo

948 to fall off — caerse de

951 famous actress — Maricarmen es una actriz muy **famosa**.

952 fan — el ventilador

953 fancy clothes — trajes **elegantes, de fantasía**

954 fang — el colmillo

La ciudad está **lejos**.
955   The city is **far** away.

¡Que te vaya bien!
956   Farewell !

En **las granjas** se cultiva la tierra.
957   farm

el granjero
958   farmer

rápido, veloz
959   fast

Yo siempre **me abrocho** el cinturón de seguridad.
960   I **fasten** my seatbelt.

Al **gordo** Hernán le gustan los dulces.
961   fat

Ingerir substancias venenosas es **mortal**.
962   fatal

el padre
963   father

Esta **llave** gotea.
964   faucet/tap*

Los dos se echan **la culpa**.
965   Whose **fault** is it?

el favor
¿Te puedo pedir **un favor**? Marisol es buena persona y le gusta hacer **favores**.
Can I ask you a favor? Marisol is nice and likes doing people favors.
966   favor/favour*

mi helado **favorito**
967   favorite/favourite*

¿Quién le **tiene miedo** al lobo?
968   to **fear** the worst

el festín
969   feast

Antiguamente **las plumas** se usaban para escribir.
970   feather

Febrero es el segundo mes del año.
971   February

Juanita **alimenta** al bebé cada cuatro horas.
972   to **feed**

Me siento muy bien.
973   I **feel** well.

La hembra es la que pone los huevos.
974   female

la cerca, la reja, la valla, la verja

975   fence

el guardafango, el tapabarro

976   fender/wing*

el helecho

977   fern

el transbordador

978   ferry

el festival

979   festival

Pobre Jorge, tiene mucha **fiebre**.

980   fever

Vino **poca** gente.

981   Few people came.

un campo

982   field

Eliana es la **quinta** del grupo.

983   fifth

Estos dos se llevan mal y no hacen más que **pelear**.

984   to fight

limar, limarse

985   to file

llenar

986   to fill

un rollo de **película**

988   film

Este cerdo **inmundo** no se baña jamás.

989   filthy

la aleta de tiburón

990   fin

llenar

987   to fill up

una **multa** por exceso de velocidad

991   fine

Estoy **bien**.

992   I am fine.

el dedo

993   finger

las huellas digitales, las huellas dactilares

994   fingerprint

terminar

995   to finish

De **los abetos** se saca la trementina.

996   fir

el fuego, el incendio

997   fire

el camión de bomberos, la bomba, el carrobomba

998   fire engine

la escalera de incendio

999   fire escape

el petardo

1000   firecracker/banger*

el bombero

1001   firefighter

la chimenea, el hogar

1002   fireplace

firme, la firma

Marisol me dio un **firme** apretón de manos.
La firma de Lucía fabrica juguetes.
El abuelo se puso **firme** y no quiere que Martín tome otro helado más.

Marisol gave me a firm handshake.
Lucia's firm makes toys.
Grandpa's decision is firm, Martin cannot have another ice cream.

1003   firm

el primero de la fila

1004   first

Los pescados vivos se llaman **peces**.

1005   fish

pescar

1006   to fish

el anzuelo

1007   fishhook

el puño

1008   fist

el número cinco

1009   five

¿Crees tú que lo puede **arreglar**?

1010   to fix

la bandera pirata

1011   flag

los copos de nieve

1012   flake

la llama

1013   flame

¿Por qué **aleteas** tanto, pajarito?

1014   to flap

Las luces de bengala sirven para hacer señales.

1015   flare

el fogonazo

1016   flash

la linterna

1017   flashlight/torch*

el frasco

1018   flask

plano, liso

1019   flat

El uslero sirve para **aplanar** la masa.

1020   to flatten

¿Qué **sabor** te gusta más?

1021   flavor/flavour*

Capitán tiene **una pulga** en el lomo.

1022   flea

Roberto **huyó** al ver al marciano.

1023   to flee

el vellón

1024   fleece

Este caballero es bastante entrado en **carnes**.

1025   flesh

flotar

1026   to float

la bandada de pájaros

1027   flock

la inundación

1028   flood

el suelo, el piso

1029   floor

De **la harina** sale el pan.

1030   flour

La sangre **corre** hacia la vena.

1031   to flow

la flor

1032   flower

Luis está en cama con **influenza**.

1033   flu

la pelusa

1034   fluff

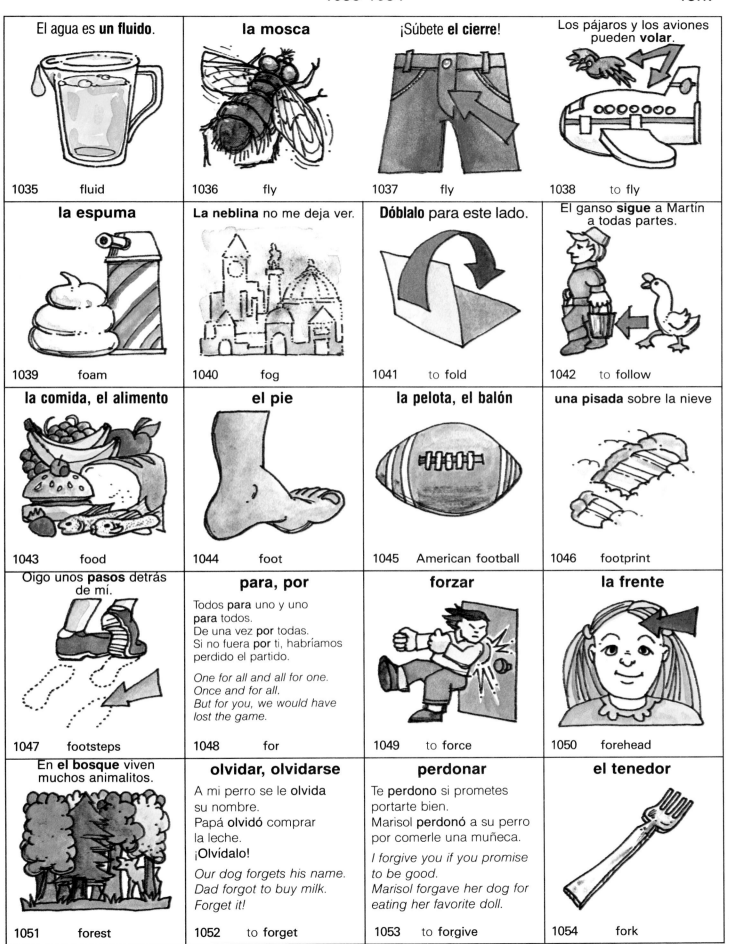

El agua es **un fluido**.

1035   fluid

la mosca

1036   fly

¡Súbete **el cierre**!

1037   fly

Los pájaros y los aviones pueden **volar**.

1038   to fly

la espuma

1039   foam

La neblina no me deja ver.

1040   fog

Dóblalo para este lado.

1041   to fold

El ganso **sigue** a Martín a todas partes.

1042   to follow

la comida, el alimento

1043   food

el pie

1044   foot

la pelota, el balón

1045   American football

una pisada sobre la nieve

1046   footprint

Oigo unos **pasos** detrás de mí.

1047   footsteps

para, por

Todos **para** uno y uno **para** todos.
De una vez **por** todas.
Si no fuera **por** ti, habríamos perdido el partido.

One for all and all for one.
Once and for all.
But for you, we would have lost the game.

1048   for

forzar

1049   to force

la frente

1050   forehead

En **el bosque** viven muchos animalitos.

1051   forest

olvidar, olvidarse

A mi perro se le **olvida** su nombre.
Papá **olvidó** comprar la leche.
¡**Olvídalo**!

Our dog forgets his name.
Dad forgot to buy milk.
Forget it!

1052   to forget

perdonar

Te **perdono** si prometes portarte bien.
Marisol **perdonó** a su perro por comerle una muñeca.

I forgive you if you promise to be good.
Marisol forgave her dog for eating her favorite doll.

1053   to forgive

el tenedor

1054   fork

la grúa de horquilla

1055   forklift

el maniquí

1056   form/tailor's dummy*

A cargo del **fuerte** está la guarnición.

1057   fort

adelante, atrevido, avanzado

¿Quién quiere salir **adelante**?
Marisol opina que el tipo es muy **atrevido**.
Las tropas están en posición **avanzada**.

Who would like to come forward?
Marisol thinks he is
too forward.
The troops are in a forward
position.

1058   forward

Los restos **fósiles** de un pescado.

1059   fossil

un olor **fétido**

1060   foul odor/odour*

los cimientos de una casa

1061   foundation

la fuente

1062   fountain

Los zorros son muy astutos.

1063   fox

una fracción del pastel

1064   fraction

Los huevos son muy **frágiles**.

1065   fragile

el marco

1066   frame

pocas **pecas**

1067   freckle

libre

1068   free

A Inuk se le **congeló** el refresco.

1069   to freeze

una manzana **fresca**, recién cortada

1070   fresh

el viernes

El amigo de Róbinson Crusoe se llamaba igual que el día **viernes**.

Robinson Crusoe's friend
was named after this day.

1071   Friday

Algunos lo llaman **refrigerador**, otros **nevera**.

1072   fridge

las amigas

1073   friends

A María le encanta **asustar** a su hermano.

1074   to frighten

La rana es un batracio.

1075   frog

Yo vengo **del** planeta Marte.

1076   I am **from** Mars.

la parte de adelante

1077   front

¿Ves **la escarcha** en la ventana?

1078   frost

¿Por qué **frunces el ceño**?

1079   to frown

La fruta es mucho mejor que los caramelos.

1080   fruit

freír

1081   to fry

la sartén

1082   frying pan

Los autos funcionan con **combustible**.

1083   Cars need **fuel**.

lleno, colmado

1084   full

diversión, entretenimiento

1085   having **fun**

un fondo de ayuda para las personas necesitadas

1086   charity **fund**

Cuando muere alguien se hace **un funeral**.

1087   funeral

¿Conoces la ley del **embudo**?

1088   funnel

gracioso, divertido, raro

Ese es un payaso muy **gracioso**.
Me pasó algo muy **divertido** camino de la escuela.
Marisol se sintió muy **rara** después de comer champiñones.

That's a very funny clown.
A funny thing happened on the way to school.
Marisol felt funny after eating that mushroom.

1089   funny

¿Un abrigo de **pieles** en pleno verano?

1090   fur coat

Mi casa se calienta con **una caldera**.

1092   furnace/boiler*

los muebles

1093   furniture

¿Se quemaron **los fusibles**?

1094   fuse

Micifuz es un gatito muy **lanudo**.

1091   furry

Un ventarrón es un viento muy fuerte.

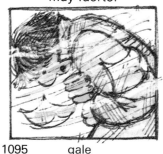

1095   gale

la galería de arte

1096   gallery

Los caballos caminan, trotan y **galopan**.

1097   to gallop

A Pablo le encantan **los juegos**.

1098   game

El ganso es macho, la gansa es hembra.

1099   gander

la pandilla de ladrones

1100   gang

Marisol tiene **un hueco** entre los dientes.

1101   gap

El auto está guardado en **la cochera**.

1102   garage

la basura

1103   garbage/rubbish*

el cubo, el tacho o tarro de la basura

1104   garbage can/rubbish bin*

la huerta, el jardín

1105   vegetable **garden**

hacer gárgaras

1106   to gargle

El ajo tiene un sabor muy fuerte.

1107   garlic

Las ligas sirven para afirmar las medias.

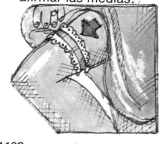

1108   garter

el gas

Algunos globos se inflan con **gas**.
Hay **gases** que son más livianos que el aire.
Los bomberos usan máscara de **gas** para protegerse del humo.

The balloon was filled with gas.
Some gases are lighter than air.
Firemen wear gas masks against the smoke.

1109   gas

Algunos la llaman **gasolina**, otros **bencina**.

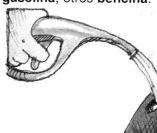

1110   gas/petrol*

El pedal de la bencina se llama **acelerador**.

1111 gas pedal/accelerator*

la bomba de gasolina

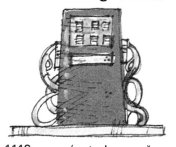

1112   gas/petrol pump*

la gasolinera, la estación de servicio

1113   gas/petrol station*

la puerta, el portón

1114   gate

Esta señora está **recogiendo** flores.

1115   to gather

los engranajes

1116   gears

la piedra preciosa, la gema

1117   gem

Los generales están muy generalizados.

1118   general

un amigo **generoso**

1119   a generous friend

una persona **bondadosa**

1120   a gentle person

Mi papá es todo un **caballero**.

1121   gentleman

un cerdo **legítimo**

1122   a genuine pig

En las escuelas se estudia **la geografía**.

1123   geography

el geranio

1124   geranium

Los gerbos son unos roedores muy simpáticos.

1125   gerbil

Los gérmenes causan muchas enfermedades.

1126   germ

¡Micifuz, **agarra** ese ratón!

1127   Get that mouse!

Quiero que me **devuelvas** mi libro.

1128   I want to get it back.

Marisol **se mete** despacito.

1129   to get in the pool

Marisol **se baja** . . .

1130   to get off

. . . y **se sube**.

1131   to get on

Sale a **botar** la basura . . .

1132   to get rid of

. . . pero primero **se levanta**.

1133   to get up

¿Le tienes miedo a **los fantasmas**?

1134   ghost

el gigante

1135   giant

el regalo, el obsequio

1136   gift

una ballena **gigantesca**

1137   gigantic

reírse tontamente

1138   to giggle

Los peces tienen muchas **agallas**.

1139   gills

El jengibre se usa para cocinar.

1140   ginger

una figurita de **pan de jengibre**

1141   gingerbread

Los gitanos siempre viajan en caravanas.

1142   gipsy

¿Sabes por qué **las jirafas** no usan corbata?

1143   giraffe

la niña

1144   girl

Yo le **di** mi paraguas porque ella no tenía.

1145   to give

el glaciar

1148   glacier

Me **alegro**.

1149   I am glad.

Las ventanas se hacen de **vidrio**.

1150   glass

Cuando escampó, ella me lo **devolvió**.

1146   to give back

¿Tú usas **anteojos**?

1152   glasses

deslizarse

1153   to glide

el vaso de agua

1151   glass

¡Me **rindo**!

1147   I give up!

el planeador	**los guantes**	**La goma** sirve para pegar.	**ir**
1154 glider	1155 gloves	1156 glue	1157 to go
El arquero defiende **el arco**.	Algunas **cabras** son domésticas, otras no.	**Los lentes protectores** se usan para nadar.	El técnico **baja** a hacer su trabajo.
1161 goal	1162 goat	1163 goggles	1158 to go down
la barra de **oro**	Yo me río de **los peces de colores**.	El Tío Lalo es muy bueno para **el golf**.	Capitán **entró** a dormir una siesta.
1164 gold	1165 goldfish	1166 golf	1159 to go in
una **buena** comida	¡**Adiós,** mamá!	**la gansa**	Juanito **subió** por la mata de frijoles.
1167 good	1168 Goodbye!	1169 goose	1160 to go up
la grosella silvestre	Esta señora se cree **muy hermosa**.	**el gorila**	**gobernar**
1170 gooseberry	1171 gorgeous	1172 gorilla	El gobierno **gobierna** el país. **Gobernar** un país no es tan fácil como parece. *The government governs the country. It is not as easy to govern a country as it seems.* 1173 to **govern**

el gobierno

Al **gobierno** lo elige el pueblo.
El papá de Marisol es un almirante y trabaja para **el gobierno**.

The government is elected by the people.
Marisol's dad, the admiral, works for the government.

1174   government

arrebatar

1175   to grab

Él es muy gentil.

1176   He is very gracious.

Estoy en primer grado.

1177   grade / form*

El grano cosechado se guarda en los graneros.

1178   grain

1000 **gramos** = 1 kilo

1179   gram

el nieto, la nieta

1180   grandchild

el abuelo

1181   grandfather

A la **abuela** de Marisol le gusta tocar la batería.

1182   grandmother

El granito es una piedra muy dura.

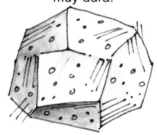

1183   granite

otorgar, conceder

Le voy a **otorgar** diez días de licencia.
Tu hada madrina te va a **conceder** tres deseos.

I grant you ten days' leave of absence.
The good fairy will grant you three wishes.

1184   to grant

un racimo de uvas

1185   grapes

---

la toronja, el pomelo

1186   grapefruit

el gráfico

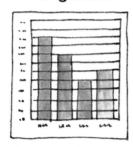

1187   graph

el césped, el pasto, la hierba

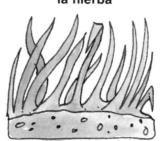

1188   grass

el saltamontes

1189   grasshopper

---

el rallador

1190   grater

la tumba, la sepultura

1191   grave

Siempre hay **ripio** a la orilla del camino.

1192   gravel

La fuerza de **gravedad** hace que la manzana caiga.

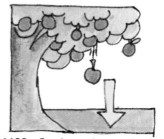

1193   Gravity makes apples fall.

Las vaquitas salieron a **pastar.** **1194** to graze	Con un poco de **grasa** se acaban los ruidos. **1195** grease	un **magnífico** juguete **1196** a great toy	**avaricioso, codicioso** **1197** greedy
Verde, que te quiero **verde** . . . **1198** green	**los porotos, los frijoles, las habichuelas, las judías** **1199** green bean	**el invernadero** **1200** greenhouse	Martín siempre **saluda** a las damas. **1201** to greet
el gris **1202** grey*/gray	**asar a la parrilla** **1203** to grill	**mugriento** **1204** grimy	Jesús **sonríe** porque está contento. **1205** to grin
Mamá **muele** carne para la comida. **1206** to grind/to mince*	**Agárrate** del manubrio con fuerza. **1207** to grip	**quejarse** **1208** to groan	**El almacenero** de mi barrio es buena persona. **1209** grocer
la novia y **el novio** **1211** groom	**el mozo de cuadra, el palafrenero** **1212** groom	Gabriela **se acicala** frente al espejo. **1213** to groom	En la tienda de **abarrotes** se compran **los comestibles.** **1210** shopping for **groceries**

la acanaladura, la estría, la ranura, el surco

1214   groove

¡Qué monstruo más repugnante!

1215   gross/disgusting*

el suelo, la tierra

1216   ground

la marmota

1217   groundhog

el grupo de gente

1218   group

¿Ves cómo **crece** la planta?

1219   to grow

gruñir

1220   to growl

una persona mayor

1221   grown-up

montar guardia, vigilar

1222   to guard

adivina, buen adivinador . . .

1223   to guess

Igor le abrió la puerta al **huésped** . . .

1224   guest

. . . y lo **condujo** a su habitación.

1225   to guide

culpable

Marisol dice que no es **culpable**.
¿Quién es **culpable** de este robo?
El ladrón se declaró **culpable**.

Marisol says she is not guilty.
Who is guilty of this theft?
The thief pleaded guilty.

1226   guilty

Los conejillos de Indias comen a la carta.

1227   guinea pig

la guitarra

1228   guitar

el Golfo de México

1229   Gulf of Mexico

Las gaviotas viven cerca del agua.

1230   gull

Encías sanas, dientes sanos.

1231   gum

Mascar **chicle** es pésima costumbre.

1232   gum/chewing gum*

El agua corre por **la cuneta.**

1233   gutter

una mala **costumbre**

1234   bad habit

El abadejo es un tipo de bacalao.

1235   haddock

una tempestad de **granizo**

1236   hail

La hermana de Marisol tiene **una cabellera** abundante.

1237   hair

el cepillo para el pelo

1238   hairbrush

el peluquero, el peinador

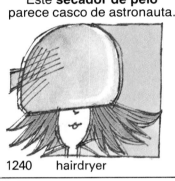

1239   hairdresser

Este **secador de pelo** parece casco de astronauta.

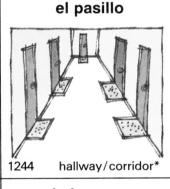

1240   hairdryer

¿Quieres **la mitad?**

1241   half

el vestíbulo

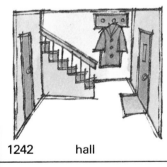

1242   hall

La noche de **Halloween** las brujas hacen un aquelarre.

1243   Halloween/Hallowe'en*

el pasillo

1244   hallway/corridor*

Al llegar a la garita nos **detuvo** un guardia.

1245   to halt

el martillo

1246   hammer

Gonzalo **martillea** de lo lindo.

1247   to hammer

la hamaca

1248   hammock

El hámster es chico y abunda en Europa.

1249   hamster

la mano

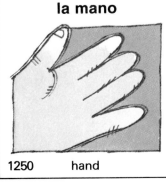

1250   hand

repartir, distribuir

1251   to hand out

el freno de mano

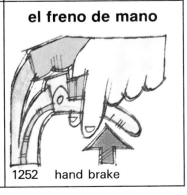

1252   hand brake

Estas **esposas** no se casan con nadie.

1253   handcuffs

**el impedimento,
el obstáculo**

La ceguera es un impedimento.
Pero las personas pueden vencer cualquier **obstáculo**.

*Being blind is a handicap.
People can overcome any handicap.*

1254   handicap

la manija, la manilla

1255   handle

**el pasamanos,
la baranda**

1256   handrail

**apuesto, guapo, bien
parecido**

1257   handsome

un tipo **diestro, hábil**

1258   handy person

¡Cuelga bien el cuadro!

1259   to hang

aferrarse, agarrarse

1260   to hang on

el hangar

1262   hangar

Cuelga tu abrigo
en este **colgador.**

1263   hanger

el pañuelo

1264   handkerchief

colgar

1261   to hang up

A todos nos puede **pasar**
un accidente.

1265   Accidents happen.

Silvio está **contento,**
pero su hermana no.

1266   He is happy.

Los buques están anclados
en **el puerto.**

1267   harbor/harbour*

No lc puedo romper,
está muy **duro.**

1268   hard

la liebre

1269   hare

¡Nunca le **hagas daño**
a un animalito!

1270   to harm

la armónica

1271   harmonica

Los caballos usan
un arnés.

1272   harness

el arpa

1273   harp

El invierno pasado fue muy **crudo**.

1274   a **harsh** winter

Don Segundo **cosechando** el trigo.

1275   to **harvest**

el sombrero

1276   hat

Los pollitos **empollan** en 21 días.

1277   to **hatch**

la hachuela

1278   hatchet

Luis el filibustero **acarreando** el botín.

1279   to **haul**

una casa **embrujada, encantada**

1280   haunted house

A Pepita le gustaría **tener** la misma muñeca.

1281   to **have**

el halcón

1282   hawk

heno para los caballos

1283   hay

Los días de **bruma** no se puede ver bien.

1284   **Haze** makes for a hazy day.

el avellano

1285   hazel

la avellana

1286   hazelnut

la cabeza

1287   head

Tengo un terrible **dolor de cabeza**.

1288   I have a **headache**.

la cabecera, el reposacabeza

1289   headrest

La pierna rota ya está **sanando**.

1290   to **heal**

Una flor **lozana**, otra marchita.

1291   **healthy** flower

un montón de basura

1292   heap/pile*

Oigo una voz.

1293   I hear a voice.

el corazón

1294   heart

calentar

1295   to heat

el calefactor, el aparato de calefacción

1296   heater/radiator*

levantar, alzar en vilo

1297   to heave

el cielo

1298   heaven

un elefante **pesado**

1299   one **heavy** elephant

¿Quién sabe podar **el seto**?

1300   hedge

Un erizo no es lo mismo que un puercoespín.

1301   hedgehog

el talón

1302   heel

el helicóptero

1303   helicopter

el infierno

1304   hell

¡Hola!

1305   hello

El rumbo se cambia con un golpe de **timón**.

1306   helm

Los soldados usan **cascos**.

1307   helmet

A la mamá de Marisol también le gusta **ayudar**.

1308   to help

Los recién nacidos son **indefensos**.

1309   helpless

la bastilla, el ruedo

1310   hem

el hemisferio

1311   hemisphere

la gallina

1312   hen

Un heptágono
tiene siete lados.

1313   heptagon

las hierbas o yerbas

1314   herbs

un rebaño de vacas

1315   herd

¡Ven aquí!

1316   Come here!

Los ermitaños
no tienen teléfono.

1317   hermit

el héroe

1318   hero

la heroína

1319   heroine

el arenque

1320   herring

Jorge **titubea**
antes de zambullirse.

1321   to hesitate

Un hexágono
tiene seis lados.

1322   hexagon

Los osos **hibernan**
todo el invierno.

1323   to hibernate

tener hipo, hipar

1324   to hiccup/hiccough*

El cuero de un animal es
lo mismo que tu piel.

1325   hide

esconderse

1326   to hide

el escondite

1327   hiding-place

una montaña muy **alta**

1328   a high mountain

**un edificio
de varios pisos**

1329   highrise/tower block*

**el liceo,
la escuela secundaria**

1330 high school/secondary school*

**la carretera,
la autopista**

1331   highway/motorway*

Secuestrar un avión es
muy feo.

1332   to hijack a plane

Sobre **la colina** hay un arbolito.

1333   hill

la bisagra, el gozne

1334   hinge

las patas traseras

1335   hind legs

mano en **cadera**

1336   hand on hip

A **los hipopótamos** no les da hipo.

1337   hippopotamus

Yo estudio **historia**.

1338   I study history.

Para clavar bien tienes que **golpear** con fuerza.

1339   to hit

Las abejas viven en **colmenas**.

1340   hive

acaparar

1341   to hoard

Hoy grité hasta quedar **ronco**.

1342   hoarse voice

Tejer es **el pasatiempo** de mamá.

1343   hobby

Mi hermano es jugador de **hockey**.

1344   hockey/ice hockey*

la azada, el azadón

1347   hoe

Marisol **sostiene** en el aire a Micifuz.

1348   to hold

Pero no está bien **sujetarlo** de esa forma.

1349   to hold down

el tejo de hockey

1345   hockey puck

el agujero, el hoyo

1350   hole

Orlando se merece unas **vacaciones**.

1351   holiday

Las ardillas viven en troncos **huecos**.

1352   hollow tree

el bastón de hockey

1346   hockey stick

El acebo se usa como adorno de Navidad.

1353   holly

En la India las vacas son **sagradas**.

1354   a holy cow

Las ardillas están **en casa**.

1355   home

las tareas, los deberes

1356   homework

¿Será un tipo **honrado**?

1357   Is he honest?

A los osos les encanta **la miel**.

1358   honey

el panal

1359   honeycomb

el melón

1360   honeydew melon

tocar la bocina

1361   to honk

graduado con **distinción**

1362   honor/honour*

El abrigo de Marisol tiene **una capucha**.

1363   hood

Para ver el motor hay que levantar **el capó**.

1364   hood/bonnet*

Los caballos tienen **cascos**.

1365   hoof

el anzuelo

1366   hook

¡Salta por **el aro**!

1367   jump through a hoop

brincar

1368   to hop

Espero ganar.

1369   I hope to win.

un mal jinete **sin remedio**

1370   hopeless

la rayuela, la reina mora, la pata coja, el luche, el piso

1371   hopscotch/hop-scotch*

El sol se levanta en **el horizonte**.

1372   horizon

horizontal

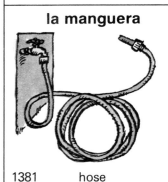

1373   horizontal

la bocina

1374   horn

el corno francés

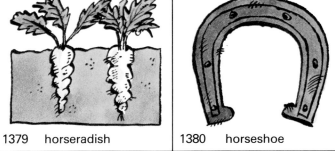

1375   French horn

el cuerno

1376   horn

Las avispas pican muy fuerte.

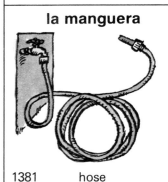

1377   hornet

el caballo

1378   horse

¿Te gustan **los rábanos picantes**?

1379   horseradish

La herradura da suerte.

1380   horseshoe

la manguera

1381   hose

el hospital

1382   hospital

Un día muy **caluroso**.

1383   hot

Los niños no deben comer cosas muy **picantes**.

1384   hot

Los hoteles dan alojamiento a los viajeros.

1386   hotel

Una hora tiene sesenta minutos.

1387   hour

el reloj de arena

1388   hourglass

Para comer **ají** hay que tener mucho cuidado.

1385   hot pepper

la casa

1389   house

el aerodeslizador

1390   hovercraft

Déjame mostrarte **cómo** se hace.

1391   I will show you **how**.

aullar

1392   to howl

el tapacubos

1393   hub cap

el arándano

1394   huckleberry

apiñarse, amontonarse

1395   to huddle

enorme

1396   huge

el casco

1397   hull

el colibrí, el picaflor

1398   hummingbird

la joroba, la giba

1399   hump

cien, ciento

1400   hundred

Tiene mucha **hambre.**

1401   She is **hungry.**

cazar

1402   to hunt

lanzar, arrojar

1403   to hurl

¿Quién será el que bautiza a **los huracanes**?

1404   hurricane

apresurarse, apurarse, darse prisa

1405   to hurry

Me **duele** la muñeca.

1406   My wrist **hurts.**

Este es mi **marido.**

1407   husband

la choza

1408   hut

el aparador, la alacena

1409   hutch/sideboard*

el jacinto

1410   hyacinth

El coro cantó **el himno** nacional.

1411   hymn

el guión

El **guión** sirve para separar palabras compuestas.

Hyphens are short lines between words that belong together.

1412   hyphen

Dos cubos de **hielo** en un vaso.

1413   ice

el helado

1414   ice cream

Los témpanos de hielo son un peligro para la navegación.

1415   iceberg

el carámbano

1416   icicle

el decorado de una torta

1417   icing

¡Se me acaba de ocurrir **una idea**!

1418   idea

Los gemelos son **idénticos.**

1419   identical twins

el idiota

1420   idiot

ocioso, inactivo

1421   idle

si

Si tuviera un martillo, clavaría donde no molestara a nadie.
Te lo compraría si pudiera.

If I had a hammer, I would only hammer when no one is sleeping.
I would buy it for you if I could.

1422   if

el iglú

1423   igloo

la llave de encendido o contacto

1424   ignition key

Jorge lleva varios días **enfermo.**

1425   ill

iluminar, alumbrar

1426   to illuminate

la ilustración

Las imágenes de un libro se llaman **ilustraciones.**
Este diccionario tiene muchas **ilustraciones.**

Pictures in a book are called illustrations.
This dictionary has many illustrations.

1427   illustration

importante

Este es un asunto muy **importante.**
Lo que es **importante** para Marisol quizás no sea **importante** para Martín.

This is an important matter.
What is important to Marisol may not be important to Martin.

1428   important

en, de

Pancho está en el hospital.
Esta sala tiene cuatro metros, **de** largo.
Marisol está vestida **de** blanco.

Pancho is in hospital.
This room is four metres in length.
Marisol is dressed in white.

1429   in

El incienso se quema en un incensario.

1430   incense

Doce **pulgadas** equivalen a un pie.

1431   inch

el índice

Al final de este libro encontrarás **un índice**. Ese **índice** contiene todas las palabras que aparecen en este diccionario.

There is an index at the back of the book.
The index contains all the words in this dictionary.

1432   index

el añil, el índigo

1433   indigo

dentro de la casa

1434   indoors

la criatura

1435   infant

Tía Tita se pescó **una infección**.

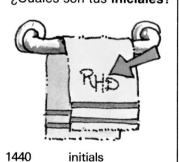

1436   infection

infeccioso, contagioso

Su estado es **infeccioso**. Cualquiera puede agarrar una enfermedad **infecciosa**. Papá tiene una risa **contagiosa**.

Her condition is infectious.
You could catch an infectious disease.
Dad has an infectious laugh.

1437   infectious

Delatar a alguien es indigno.

1438   to inform

Este oso **habita** en una cueva.

1439   The bear **inhabits** a cave.

¿Cuáles son tus **iniciales**?

1440   initials

El doctor me puso **una inyección**.

1441   injection

la herida

1442   injury

la tinta

1443   ink

Existen muchos tipos de **insectos**.

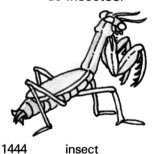

1444   insect

Este niño está **dentro** de la caja.

1445   inside

Perdona que **insista,** pero . . .

1446   to insist

inspeccionar

1447   to inspect

Usa una cuchara **en lugar de** un tenedor.

1449   Use a spoon **instead** of a fork!

la enseñanza

1450   instruction

el instructor, el profesor, el maestro

1451   instructor

el inspector

1448   inspector

el aislante, el aislamiento

Las murallas de mi casa tienen **aislante** para que no entre el frío. Los cables eléctricos tienen **aislamiento** para que no nos dé la corriente.

There is insulation in the walls of the house.
There is insulation around the wires so people will not get a shock.

1452   insulation

la intersección, el cruce

1453   intersection/crossroads*

la entrevista

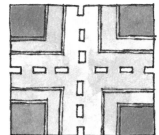

1454   interview

Domingo entró **a** su cuarto.

1455   into the room

Liliana me **presentó** a sus amigos.

1456   to introduce

Los vikingos **invadieron** muchos países.

1457   to invade

Con tanta guerra, algunos quedaron **inválidos**.

1458   invalid

¿Quién habrá **inventado** los árboles?

1459   to invent

¿Has visto al hombre **invisible**?

1460   invisible

Alguien me trajo **una invitación**.

1461   invitation

El que **invita** es él.

1462   He is inviting her.

el lirio

1463   iris

Pancho siempre **plancha** toda su ropa.

1464   to iron

la plancha

1465   iron

el yelmo de **hierro**

1466   iron mask

la isla

1467   island

la picazón, la comezón

Marisol tocó una ortiga y ahora tiene una terrible **picazón**.
La comezón desaparece siempre y cuando no te rasques.

Marisol got a bad itch from poison ivy.
The itch will go away if she does not scratch.

1468   itch

picar

1469   to itch

Me pica todo el cuerpo.

1470   My skin is **itchy**.

La hiedra
sube por las paredes.

1471   ivy

J

Enrique me **dio un codazo**.
1472 to jab

Como verán, esta **chaqueta** no es mía . . .
1473 jacket

el forro, la sobrecubierta
1474 dust jacket

un borde **mellado, dentado**
1475 jagged edge

la cárcel
1476 jail/gaol*

la mermelada
1477 jam

atascar
1478 to jam

Enero es el primer mes del año.
1479 January

el jarro, el pote, el frasco
1480 jar

Los tiburones tienen unas **mandíbulas** horribles.
1481 jaw

el pantalón vaquero, los jeans
1482 jeans

el jeep, el yip, el jip
1483 jeep

De postre tenemos **jalea**.
1484 jelly

motor a **chorro**, motor a **reacción**
1485 jet engine

avión a reacción, avión a chorro
1486 jet plane

la joya, la alhaja
1488 jewel

el rompecabezas
1489 jigsaw puzzle

Ricardo está haciendo **un trabajo**.
1490 doing a job

un chorro de agua
1487 jet of water

Un jockey es **un jinete** de caballos de carrera.

1491　　jockey

trotar

1492　　to jog

Hay que **juntar** las dos partes.

1493　　to join

la articulación del codo

1494　　joint

El pesado de Torcuato cree que sus **bromas** son buenas.

1495　　joke

El juez va a dictar su fallo.

1496　　judge

el malabarista

1497　　juggler

el jugo, el zumo de naranja

1498　　juice

¿Es **julio** buena época para ir a nadar?

1499　　July

saltar

1500　　to jump

saltar a

1501　　to jump in

saltar a

1502　　to jump on

Cristián es buen **saltador**.

1503　　jumper

el jumper, el mono

1504　　jumper/pinafore*

los cables de cierre o **puente**

1505　　jumper cables/jump leads*

En **junio** juego al tenis.

1506　　June

En **la selva** quedan pocos tigres.

1507　　jungle

Un junco es un barco chino.

1508　　junk

Los desechos quiere decir la basura.

1509　　junk

acabar de, sólo, justo

Marisol **acaba de** llegar a casa.
Sólo un poquito, gracias.
Este juez es un hombre **justo**.

Marisol just got home.
Just a little, thanks.
The judge is a just person.

1510　　just

el caleidoscopio

1511   kaleidoscope

el canguro

1512   kangaroo

la quilla

1513   keel

A Macabeo le gusta su **perrera**.

1514   kennel

el grano

1515   kernel

la tetera, la pava

1516   kettle

la llave

1517   key

patear, dar un puntapié

1518   to kick

Este **chiquillo** es amigo mío.

1519   kid

Las cabras recién nacidas se llaman **cabritos**.

1520   kid

El que **secuestra** a una persona es un criminal.

1521   to kidnap

el riñón

1522   kidney

Un cazador furtivo **mató** al pobre león.

1523   to kill

Los cacharros de greda se cuecen en **un horno**.

1524   kiln

1 **kilogramo** = 1000 gramos

1525   kilogram

1 **kilómetro** = 1000 metros

1526   kilometer/kilometre*

el faldellín escocés

1527   kilt

Un vestido es **un tipo** de ropa.

1528   A dress is a **kind** of garment.

una niñita muy **amable**

1529   **kind** girl

el rey

1530 king

el martín pescador

1531 kingfisher

el quiosco de la esquina

1532 kiosk

el pescado ahumado

1533 kippers

besar, besarse

1534 to kiss

el beso

1535 kiss

la cocina

1536 kitchen

el volantín, el papalote, el barrilete, la cometa

1537 kite

Los gatitos son muy retozones.

1538 kitten

El kiwi es una fruta muy sabrosa.

1539 kiwi

la rodilla

1540 knee

arrodillarse, hincarse

1541 to kneel

el cuchillo

1542 knife

Mamá me está **tejiendo** un chaleco de lana.

1543 to knit

la perilla, el pomo

1544 knob

Alguien **golpea** a la puerta.

1545 to knock

el nudo

1546 knot

saber, conocer

¿Tú **sabes** lo que eso quiere decir?
Conócete a ti mismo.

Do you know what it means?
Know yourself.

1547 to know

los nudillos

1548 knuckle

El oso **koala** vive en Australia.

1549 koala bear

La etiqueta dice que es un veneno mortal.
1550   label

el laboratorio
1551   laboratory

un cuello de **encaje**
1552   lace

la escalera de tijera
1554   ladder

el cucharón
1555   ladle

la señora, la dama
1556   lady

Orlando **se ata** los cordones.
1553   to lace

la mariquita, la chinita
1557   ladybug/ladybird*

los dedos de dama, las lenguas de gato
1558   ladyfingers

Esta es **la guarida** de un monstruo.
1559   lair

Los lagos están rodeados de tierra.
1560   lake

el cordero, el borrego
1561   lamb

Platero tiene una patita **coja**.
1562   lame

la lámpara
1563   lamp

el poste de alumbrado, el farol
1564   lamp-post

la lanza
1565   lance

la tierra firme
1566   land

aterrizar
1567   to land

el descanso, el rellano
1568   landing

landlord

el casero, el arrendador

El departamento en que vivimos es de mi **casero**.
El arrendador nos cobra un alquiler mensual.

The apartment we live in belongs to our landlord.
We pay our landlord rent every month.

1569   landlord

Algunas carreteras tienen cuatro **pistas**.

1570   lane

---

el idioma, la lengua, el lenguaje

¿Cuántos **idiomas** sabes hablar?
La lengua materna de Marisol es el castellano.
Los abogados usan **un lenguaje** muy complicado.

How many languages can you speak?
Spanish is Marisol's first language.
Lawyers use very complicated language.

1571   language

---

el farol, la lámpara

1572   lantern

---

un niño sentado en **el regazo** de su mamá

1573   lap

---

el alerce

1574   larch

---

la manteca

1575   lard

---

grande

1576   large

---

la alondra

1577   lark

---

la pestaña

1578   lash

---

el **último** pedazo

1579   the **last** piece

Algunas cosas **perduran** a través de los siglos.

1580   Some things do **last**.

Deja **cerrado con pestillo**, por favor.

1581   to latch

Llegas **retrasado**.

1582   You are late.

---

la espuma de afeitar

1583   lather

---

reír, reírse

1584   to laugh

Los Padilla bajaron a tierra en **una lancha**.

1585   launch

---

lanzar

1586   to launch

---

la plataforma de lanzamiento

1587   launchpad

---

la ropa sucia

1588   laundry/washing*

Liliana lava su ropa sucia en una **lavandería**.
1589　laundry/launderette*

la lavanda
1590　lavender

¡Respeta **la ley**!
1591　Obey the law!

¿Te gusta cortar **el césped**?
1592　lawn

poner baldosas
1594　to lay tiles

un pastel con varias **capas** de crema
1595　layer upon layer

¡Qué tipo más **holgazán**!
1596　He is lazy.

la cortadora de pasto
1593　lawn mower

Fidel **lleva** al caballo de las riendas.
1597　to lead

el jefe del grupo
1598　leader

la hoja
1599　leaf

Este balde **gotea**.
1600　to leak

Esta torre **se inclina** más todos los años.
1601　to lean

Yo **aprendo** a leer.
1602　I learn to read.

la correa, la traílla
1603　leash/lead*

Casi todos los zapatos se hacen de **cuero**.
1604　Shoes are made of leather.

Te lo **dejo** aquí.
1605　to leave

Víctor **se va**.
1606　to leave

el antepecho de mi ventana
1607　ledge of a window

el puerro
1608　leek

Al llegar a la esquina dobla a **la izquierda**.

1609   left

Yo soy **zurdo**. ¿Y tú?

1610   He is left-handed.

Todos tenemos **piernas**.

1611   leg

¿Conoces **la leyenda** de los Cíclopes?

1612   legend

el limón

1613   lemon

la limonada

1614   lemonade

Te voy a **prestar** este libro.

1615   to lend

el lente, el cristal

1616   lens

El leopardo es un felino.

1617   leopard

la malla

1618   leotard

En este montoncito hay **menos**.

1619   There is **less** here.

Este sabio me enseñó **una lección**.

1620   lesson

¡**Suéltame**! ¡**Déjame** ir!

1621   Let me go!

la primera **letra** del alfabeto

A

1622   letter of the alphabet

Marisol escribió **una carta** a su abuelita.

1623   letter

la lechuga

1624   lettuce

una superficie **nivelada**

1625   level surface

la palanca

1626   lever

Más rápido se pilla a **un mentiroso** que a un ladrón.

1627   liar

En **las bibliotecas** hay que guardar silencio.

1628   library

la matrícula, la patente, la placa

1629 licence plate/number plate*

lamer

1630 to lick

la tapa del frasco

1631 lid

Para **mentir** y comer pescado . . .

1632 to lie

Acaba de empezar su **vida**.

1634 life

el bote salvavidas

1635 lifeboat

levantar, alzar

1636 to lift

recostarse, acostarse, echarse

1633 to lie down

Enciende **la luz**.

1637 light/table lamp*

Papá **prende** una vela.

1638 to light

la ampolleta, la bombilla

1639 lightbulb

Una buena forma de **aligerar** la carga.

1640 She **lightens** the load.

el faro

1641 lighthouse

rayos y truenos

1642 lightning

el pararrayos

1643 lightning rod

A Pepita le **gustan** los gatos.

1644 to like

probable, apropiado

Lo más **probable** es que Consuelo no venga mañana.
Este es un lugar **apropiado** para pescar.

Consuelo is not likely to come tomorrow.
This is a likely place to fish.

1645 likely

Las lilas florecen en la primavera.

1646 lilac

azucenas de Semana Santa

1647 lily

una rama de árbol

1648 limb

la lima

1649   lime

el límite

Hay **un límite** de tres artículos por cliente.
El límite de velocidad es de 50 kilómetros por hora.
La gentileza de Orlando no tiene **límites**.

There is a limit of three items per customer.
The speed limit is 50 kilometers per hour.
There is no limit to Orlando's kindness.

1650   limit

Mi vecino **cojea** al andar.

1651   to limp

¿Sabes dibujar **líneas** rectas?

1652   line

la ropa blanca, la lencería, la ropa de cama

1653   linen

el transatlántico

1654   liner

Mi casaca tiene **un forro** muy abrigador.

1655   lining

enlazar

1656   to link

las hilachas, las pelusas

1657   lint

el león

1658   lion

los labios

1659   lips

el lápiz labial, la barra de labios

1660   lipstick

Tanto el agua como la leche son **líquidos**.

1661   liquid

la lista de las compras

1662   list

Están **escuchando** un recital.

1663   They are **listening**.

un litro

1664   liter/litre*

Ensuciar la calle está muy mal.

1665   to litter

una manzana **pequeña, una manzanita**

1666   a little apple

vivir

Marisol **vive** en una ciudad.
Tía María **vive** de su jubilación.
Vivir en el planeta Marte sería muy difícil.

Marisol lives in the city.
Aunt Maria lives on a pension.
It would be difficult to live on Mars.

1667   to live

vivaracha, vivaz

1668   lively

la sala, el salón, la sala de estar

1669   living room/lounge*

la lagartija

1670   lizard

Martín **cargó** el cañón.

1671   to load

Los obreros **cargan** un camión.

1672   to load

la hogaza de pan, **el pan**

1673   loaf

prestar

Emiliano le **prestó** dinero a Marisol después de que ella gastó toda su mesada.

Emiliano loaned Marisol some money because she had spent her allowance.

1674   to loan/lend*

un tipo de **langosta** . . .

1675   lobster

¿ Le echaste llave a la puerta?

1676   to lock

la locomotora

1678   locomotive

. . . y otro tipo de **langosta.**

1679   locust

un albergue en la montaña

1680   lodge/chalet*

una puerta con **cerradura**

1677   lock

el altillo, la buhardilla

1681   loft

el tronco, el leño

1682   log

la paleta, el chupetín

1683   lollipop

solitario

1684   lonely

Las jirafas tienen un cuello muy **largo**.

1685   long

mirar

1686   to look

Marisol teje una bufanda en **el telar**.

1687   loom

un lazo en la amarra

1688   loop

El reloj me queda **suelto**.	A Víctor se le **perdió** un guante.	un poco de **loción** para la piel	La música muy **fuerte** me da dolor de cabeza.
1689 loose	1690 to lose	1691 lotion	1692 loud
el altavoz, el parlante, el megáfono	**holgazanear, flojear**	**el amor** El **amor** es algo muy importante. Marisol dice que el que tiene **amor** lo tiene todo. *Love is very important.* *Marisol says that if you have love you have everything.*	Nosotros **nos queremos** mucho.
1693 loudspeaker	1694 to lounge	1695 love	1696 to love
preciosa, amorosa	una ramita **baja**	**bajar**	**afortunado** Raúl es **afortunado** de tener tan buenos amigos. ¡Qué tipo más **afortunado**! *Raul is lucky to have such good friends.* *What a lucky dog!*
1697 lovely	1698 low branch	1699 to lower	1700 lucky
el equipaje	El agua **tibia** no está ni fría ni caliente.	La mamá canta **una canción de cuna** a su bebé.	**la madera**
1701 luggage	1702 lukewarm water	1703 lullaby	1704 lumber/timber*
el chichón	**el almuerzo**	**la lonchera, la fiambrera**	Fumar daña **los pulmones**.
1705 lump	1706 lunch	1707 lunchbox	1708 lung

la revista

1709   magazine

Los gusanos no son muy agradables.

1710   maggot

un acto de **magia** un tanto diferente

1711   magic

el imán

1713   magnet

el **magnífico** manto del rey de la selva

1714   magnificent

la lupa

1715   magnifying glass

el mago

1712   magician

la urraca

1716   magpie

enviar por correo

1717   to mail/post*

el cartero

1718 mail carrier/postman*

Gustavo está **haciendo** un avioncito.

1719   to make

A Soledad le gusta usar **maquillaje**.

1720   makeup

el macho y la hembra

1721   male

el mazo

1722   mallet

el hombre y la mujer

1723   man

Al **mandarín** le gustan **las mandarinas**.

1724   mandarin

la mandolina

1725   mandolin

La melena de los caballos se llama **crin**.

1726   mane

El mango es una fruta muy dulce.

1727   mango

un señor de muy buenos **modales**

1728 He has good **manners**.

varios, muchos

1729 many

el mapa

1730 map

una escultura en **mármol**

1731 marble

marchar

1733 to march

El tercer mes del año se llama **marzo**.

1734 March

La hembra del caballo se llama **yegua**.

1735 mare

las canicas, las bolitas

1732 marbles

la caléndula

1736 marigold

Marca la respuesta que te parezca correcta.

1737 to mark

¡Sacaste muy buenas **notas**!

1738 mark

Mi papá tiene un puesto en **el mercado**.

1739 market

casarse

1740 to marry

el pantano, la ciénaga

1741 marsh

moler papas

1742 to mash potatoes

la máscara, el antifaz

1743 mask

Los fieles de la balanza tienen **masas** diferentes.

1744 mass

Todos los veleros tienen **un mástil**.

1745 mast

Carolina ya **domina** el arte de la bicicleta.

1746 to master

el partido de tenis

1747 match

Jugar con fósforos es muy peligroso.

1748　　match

---

las matemáticas

2
+2
4

1749　　mathematics

---

la cuestión, la materia

Iris vuelve en **cuestión** de minutos.
Tener **materia** gris significa ser inteligente.

Iris will be back in a matter of minutes.
To have gray matter means to be smart.

1750　　matter

---

el colchón

1751　　mattress

Mayo es el quinto mes del año.

1752　　May

---

acaso, quizás, tal vez

Acaso Marisol debiera quedarse en casa.
Quizás mamá sepa.
No te respondo ni que sí ni que no, sino que **tal vez**.

Maybe Marisol should stay home.
Maybe Mother knows.
The answer is not yes, and it is not no, it is maybe.

1753　　maybe

---

el alcalde de mi pueblo

1754　　mayor

Este es un laberinto.

1755　　maze

Los prados tienen pasto y flores.

1756　　meadow

---

el sabanero

1757　　meadowlark

---

la comida

1758　　meal

---

un tipo malo

1759　　mean person

A casi todos nos da el sarampión.

1760　　measles

---

medir

1　2　3　4　5　6

1761　　to measure

---

la carne

1762　　meat

---

el mecánico

1763　　mechanic

Mafalda se ganó una medalla al mérito.

1764　　medal

---

un remedio para el dolor de cabeza

1765　　medicine

---

mediano

1766　　medium

---

encontrarse

1767　　to meet

Todos los lunes hay **reunión** de profesores.

1768   meeting

el melón

1769   melon

derretir, derretirse

1770   to melt

Este club tiene cuatro **miembros**.

1771   Our club has four **members**.

el menú, la carta, la lista, la minuta

1772   menu

la merced, la compasión

Quedamos a **merced** de los elementos.
Ese miserable no tuvo **compasión** con nadie.

We are at the mercy of the weather.
The bandit showed no mercy to anyone.

1773   mercy

la sirena

1774   mermaid

alegre, feliz

1775   merry

¡Qué **desorden** más espantoso!

1776   a real mess

Te traigo **un mensaje**.

1777   message

el mensajero

1778   messenger

Esta es una jarra de **metal**.

1779   metal

Los meteoritos provienen del espacio.

1780   meteorite

el medidor

1781   meter

Un metro equivale a unas 40 pulgadas.

1782   meter/metre*

el método

Marisol usa **un método** para aprender más rápido.
Un método es una forma de hacer las cosas.
Sus **métodos** no son muy ortodoxos.

Marisol has a method for learning quickly.
A method is a way of doing things.
His methods are not very orthodox.

1783   method

el metrónomo

1784   metronome

Ricardo prefiere cantar con **micrófono**.

1785   microphone

el microscopio

1786   microscope

el horno de **microondas**

1787   microwave oven

el mediodía	en **el medio**	**el enano**	**la medianoche**
1788 midday	1789 in the middle	1790 midget	1791 midnight

la milla

Una milla equivale a 1,6 kilómetros.
El límite de velocidad es de 30 **millas** por hora.

One mile equals 1.6 kilometers.
The speed limit is 30 miles per hour.

1792   mile

la leche	**el molino**	**una mente** brillante
$E = MC^2$		
1793 milk	1794 mill	1795 mind

una mina subterránea	**Los mineros** trabajan duro.	**los minerales**	**el pececillo**
1796 mine	1797 miner	1798 minerals	1799 minnow

la menta, la hierbabuena	¿Cuánto es siete **menos** cinco?	**Un minuto** tiene sesenta segundos.	**Un milagro** que funcionó al revés.
	$7 - 5 = 2$		
1800 mint	1801 minus	1802 minute	1803 miracle

un espejismo en el desierto	**el espejo**	**Los avaros** no convidan a nadie.	**Extraño** tanto a mi familia.
1804 mirage	1805 mirror	1806 miser	1807 to miss

el proyectil, el misil

1808   missile

Ignacio se extravió en **la niebla**.

1809   mist

el muérdago

1810   mistletoe

los mitones

1811   mittens

mezclar

1812   to mix

la batidora

1813   mixer

Los castillos de antaño tenían **un foso**.

1814   moat

burlarse

1815   to mock

el sinsonte

1816   mockingbird

un avioncito a **escala**

1817   **model** airplane/aeroplane*

un sillón **moderno**

1818   **modern** chair

¡Este niño tiene los pañales **mojados**!

1819   moist

el topo

1820   mole

Tengo **un lunar** en la cara.

1821   mole

Un **momento**, por favor.

1822   One **moment** please.

el lunes

El **lunes** es el primer día de la semana.
Todos **los lunes** Marisol se levanta temprano.

Monday is the first day of the week.
Every Monday, Marisol gets up early.

1823   Monday

el dinero

1824   money

El mono desciende del árbol.

1825   monkey

Este es un tipo de tiburón llamado **angelote**.

1826   monkfish

el monstruo

1827   monster

El año tiene doce **meses**.
1828   month

Más vale hacer **un monumento** a la verdad.
1829   monument

de buen **humor** . . .
1830   He is in a good **mood**.

. . . y de mal **genio**
1831   He is in a bad **mood**.

la luna creciente
1832   moon

el alce
1833   moose

la mañana
1834   morning

El mortero sirve para machacar.
1835   mortar and pestle

el mosaico
1836   mosaic

el mosquito
1837   mosquito

el musgo, el moho
1838   moss

la madre
1839   mother

el motor eléctrico
1840   motor

la motocicleta, la moto
1841   motorcycle

el molde para tortas
1842   mould*/mold

un montículo de tierra
1843   mound

Cada cual **se monta** como quiere.
1844   to mount

la montaña
1845   mountain

el ratón, la laucha
1846   mouse

el bigote, el mostacho
1847   moustache*/mustache

la boca

1848 mouth

Los caracoles **se mueven** muy despacito.

1849 to move

¿Existirá la máquina de **movimiento** perpetuo?

1850 movement

el cine, el teatro

1851 movie/film*

cortar el pasto

1852 to **mow** the lawn

Esto es **mucho** para una sola persona.

1853 too **much** for me

¿Pero qué haces sentado en **el barro**?

1854 mud

la mula, el mulo

1855 mule

multiplicar

1856 multiply

las paperas

1857 mumps

Asesinar a alguien es un crimen horrendo.

1858 to murder

Los luchadores tienen grandes **músculos**.

1859 muscle

el museo

1860 museum

Algunos **hongos** son muy venenosos.

1861 mushroom

Marisol es muy aficionada a **la música**.

1862 music

La mamá de Marisol es **músico**.

1863 musician

Los mejillones son invertebrados.

1864 mussel

Usted perdone, pero **tiene que** saltar. . .

1865 You **must** jump.

la mostaza

1866 mustard

el bozal

1867 muzzle

N

el clavo

1868   nail

la uña

1869   fingernail

el cortaúñas

1870   nail clipper

desnudos, en cueros, piluchos, calatos

1872   naked

Mi nombre es . . .

1873   My name is...

la servilleta

1874   napkin/serviette*

clavar

1871   to nail

Está tan angosto que no alcanzo a pasar.

1875   too narrow to pass

Una nación es lo mismo que un país.

1876   nation

natural

Comer alimentos naturales es muy bueno para la salud.
Es importante proteger los recursos naturales.
Es muy natural que llore un recién nacido.

It is healthy to eat natural foods.
It is important to protect natural resources.
It is very natural that a newborn should cry.

1877   natural

Cuida siempre la naturaleza.

1878   nature

una niña revoltosa

1879   She is naughty.

Antes se navegaba según las estrellas.

1880   to navigate

Ya está llegando cerca . . .

1881   near

pulcro, aseado

1882   neat

No es muy agradable, pero es necesario.

1883   Not pleasant, but necessary.

el cuello

1884   neck

el collar

1885   necklace

La venganza es el néctar de los dioses.

1886   nectar

**el melocotón,
el durazno pelado**

1887   nectarine

el apuro, la carencia

Marisol siempre ayuda a un
amigo en **apuros**.
En el desierto hay una gran
carencia de agua.

*Marisol always helps her
friends in need.
There is a great need for
water in the desert.*

1888   need

¡Dios mío, **necesito**
un vaso de agua!

1889   I **need** water.

¿Sabes enhebrar
una aguja?

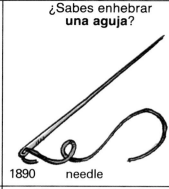

1890   needle

El que **descuida** a su
perro no merece tenerlo.

1891   He **neglects** his dog.

Las vacas mugen, los
caballos **relinchan**.

1892   to **neigh**

los vecinos

1893 neighbors/neighbours*

Ninguno de los dos
me queda bien.

1894   **neither** one fits

un letrero de neón

1895   neon sign

Mi **sobrino** es el hijo
de mi hermano.

1896 My **nephew** is my brother's son.

Los nervios son parte
del sistema nervioso.

1897   nerve

Toti se siente
un poco **nervioso**.

1898   nervous

Se ven dos huevitos
en **el nido**.

1899   nest

La ortiga
pica como diablo.

1900   nettle

¡Nunca juegues
con fuego!

1901   **Never** play with fire!

nuevo

1902   new

**la noticia, la nueva,
la novedad**

Mamá lee **las noticias**.
Tenemos buenas **nuevas**.
¿Has tenido **novedades** de
tu casa?

*Mom reads the news.
The news is good.
Any news from home?*

1903   news

el diario, el periódico

1904   newspaper

¡El siguiente!
¡El próximo!

1905   Next !

Las ardillas siempre
mordisquean la comida.

1906   to **nibble**

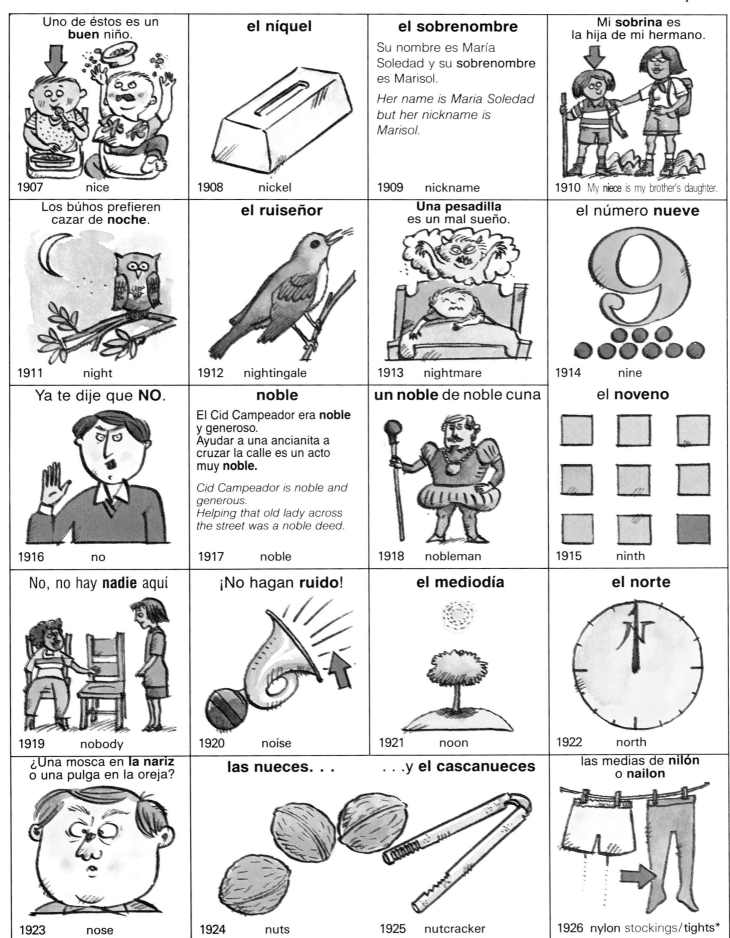

Uno de éstos es un **buen** niño.
1907   nice

el níquel
1908   nickel

el sobrenombre
Su nombre es María Soledad y su **sobrenombre** es Marisol.

Her name is Maria Soledad but her nickname is Marisol.
1909   nickname

Mi **sobrina** es la hija de mi hermano.
1910   My niece is my brother's daughter.

Los búhos prefieren cazar de **noche**.
1911   night

el ruiseñor
1912   nightingale

Una **pesadilla** es un mal sueño.
1913   nightmare

el número **nueve**
1914   nine

Ya te dije que **NO**.
1916   no

noble
El Cid Campeador era **noble** y generoso.
Ayudar a una ancianita a cruzar la calle es un acto muy **noble**.

Cid Campeador is noble and generous.
Helping that old lady across the street was a noble deed.
1917   noble

un noble de noble cuna
1918   nobleman

el **noveno**
1915   ninth

No, no hay **nadie** aquí
1919   nobody

¡No hagan **ruido**!
1920   noise

el mediodía
1921   noon

el norte
1922   north

¿Una mosca en **la nariz** o una pulga en la oreja?
1923   nose

las nueces. . .
. . .**y el cascanueces**
1924   nuts   1925   nutcracker

las medias de **nilón** o **nailon**
1926   nylon stockings/**tights***

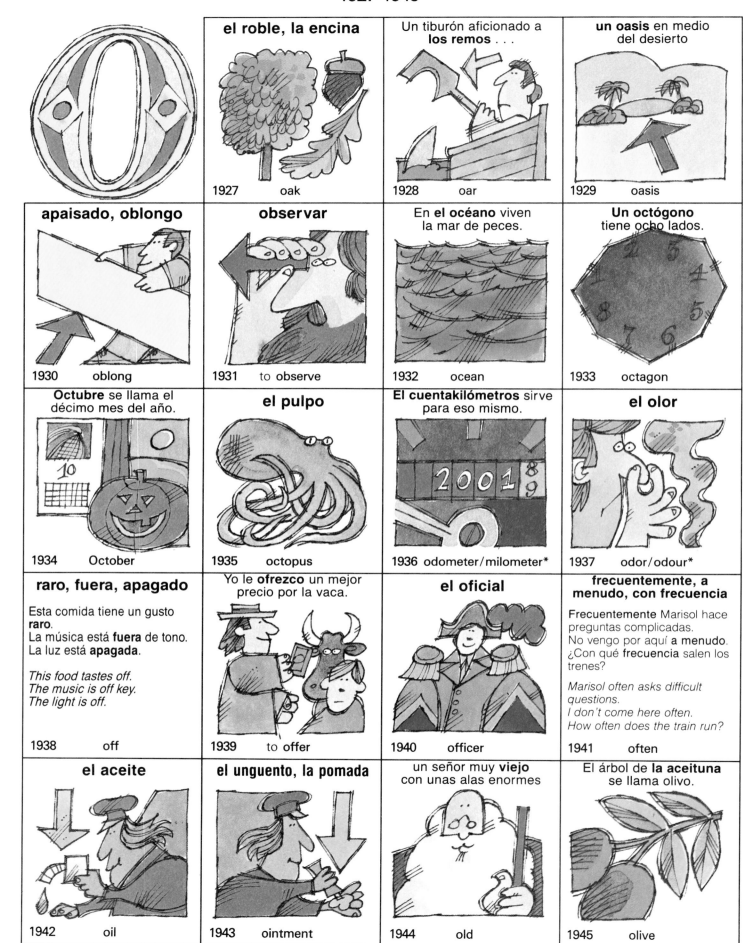

el roble, la encina

1927 oak

Un tiburón aficionado a **los remos** . . .

1928 oar

un oasis en medio del desierto

1929 oasis

apaisado, oblongo

1930 oblong

observar

1931 to observe

En **el océano** viven la mar de peces.

1932 ocean

Un octógono tiene ocho lados.

1933 octagon

Octubre se llama el décimo mes del año.

1934 October

el pulpo

1935 octopus

El cuentakilómetros sirve para eso mismo.

1936 odometer/milometer*

el olor

1937 odor/odour*

raro, fuera, apagado

Esta comida tiene un gusto **raro**.
La música está **fuera** de tono.
La luz está **apagada**.

This food tastes off.
The music is off key.
The light is off.

1938 off

Yo le **ofrezco** un mejor precio por la vaca.

1939 to offer

el oficial

1940 officer

frecuentemente, a menudo, con frecuencia

Frecuentemente Marisol hace preguntas complicadas.
No vengo por aquí **a menudo**.
¿Con qué **frecuencia** salen los trenes?

Marisol often asks difficult questions.
I don't come here often.
How often does the train run?

1941 often

el aceite

1942 oil

el unguento, la pomada

1943 ointment

un señor muy **viejo** con unas alas enormes

1944 old

El árbol de **la aceituna** se llama olivo.

1945 olive

Para hacer **una tortilla** hay que quebrar huevos. **1946** omelette	El florero está **encima de** la mesa. **1947** on the table	**una vez** Erase **una vez**, que había una niñita llamada Marisol . . . He visto esta película más de **una vez**. *Once upon a time, there was a little girl called Marisol . . .* *I have seen this movie more than once.* **1948** once	**el número uno** **1949** one
la cebolla **1950** onion	Tú eres mi **único** amor. **1951** my only love	No dejes la puerta **abierta**. **1952** open	**abrir** **1953** to open
la operación **1954** operation	**la zarigüeya** **1955** opossum	**en frente de, contrario, opuesto** Los Zenteno viven **en frente de** nosotros. El bien es **lo contrario** del mal. Cada uno partió en dirección **opuesta**. *The Zentenos live opposite us.* *Good is the opposite of bad.* *We went in opposite directions.* **1956** opposite	**o, u** ¿Puedo entrar, **o** estás ocupado? Entregue detalles sobre su profesión **u** oficio. *Can I come in or are you busy?* *Provide details about your profession or trade.* **1957** or
la naranja **1958** orange	el color **naranja, anaranjado** **1959** orange	En **los huertos** hay árboles frutales. **1960** orchard	**la orquesta** **1961** orchestra
la orquídea **1962** orchid	¿Puedo **pedir** mi comida? **1963** to order	**el orégano** **1964** oregano	**un órgano** de iglesia **1965** organ

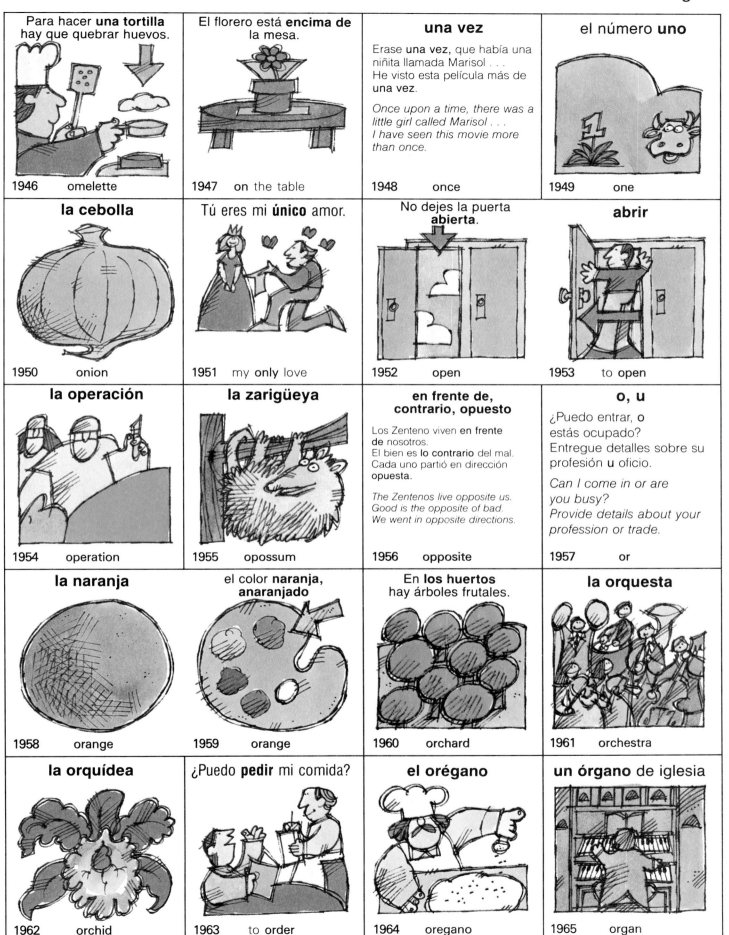

la oropéndola

1966   oriole

Un huérfano
no tiene padres.

1967   orphan

Las avestruces
no pueden volar.

1968   ostrich

Las nutrias son
muy juguetonas.

1969   otter

Una libra tiene
dieciséis **onzas**.

1970   ounce

¿A quién no le gusta andar
al **aire libre**?

1971   outdoors

¿Te gusta mi
indumentaria?

1972   outfit

ovalado

1973   oval

En la puerta del **horno**
se quema el pan.

1974   oven

¡Hombre **al agua**!

1975   Man overboard!

el **sobretodo**, el abrigo,
el gabán

1976   overcoat

**desbordar, rebosar,
derramarse**

1977   to overflow

el chanclo, la galocha

1978   overshoe

**darse vuelta de
campana, volcarse**

1979   to overturn

deber

Ustedes le **deben** respeto a
la maestra.
Lo mejor es no **deberle**
dinero a nadie.

*You owe respect to your
teacher.
It is best not to owe
any money.*

1980   to owe

la lechuza, el búho

1981   owl

tener, ser dueño de

Nosotros **tenemos** casa
propia.
Los Zenteno **son dueños
de** una cabañita cerca
del lago.

*We own our house.
The Zentenos own a
cottage on the lake.*

1982   to own

el buey

1983   ox

el oxígeno

1984   oxygen

Algunas **ostras** traen
una perla adentro.

1985   oyster

P

Marisol **empaca** su mochila:

1986   to pack

el paquete

1987   package

Alguien estuvo usando mi **bloc** de papel.

1988   pad

Georgina va remando con **un canalete** . . .

1990   paddle

. . . pero todavía no sabe **remar** muy bien.

1991   to paddle

el candado

1992   padlock

la plataforma de lanzamiento

1989   pad

Demos vuelta **la página**.

1993   page

un balde de agua para abrevar los caballos

1994   pail

la pintura

1996   paint

No es muy astuto tocar **la pintura** fresca.

1997   wet paint

Martín se lastímo un dedo y siente mucho **dolor**.

1995   pain

el pintor de brocha gorda

2000   painter

Tía Irma le pidió a Martín que **pintara** la cerca.

1998   to paint

la brocha

1999   paintbrush

la pintura, el cuadro

2001   painting

un par de zapatillas

2002   a **pair** of shoes

el palacio

2003   palace

Esta flor es de un tono más bien **pálido**.

2004   pale

la paleta	Yo conozco mi ciudad como **la palma** de mi mano.	**la fuente**	A Marisol le encantan **los panqueques**.
2005 palette	2006 palm	2007 pan	2008 pancake
el oso **panda**	**el tablero** de instrumentos	**la zampoña**	**el pensamiento**
2009 panda	2010 panel	2011 panpipe	2012 pansy
jadear, acezar	**¿La pantera** rosa?	**los pantalones**	**la papaya**
2013 to pant	2014 panther	2015 pants/trousers*	2016 papaya
el papel	**el paracaídas**	**el desfile, la parada**	**unas líneas paralelas**
2017 paper	2018 parachute	2019 parade	2020 parallel lines
El ratoncito quedó **paralizado** de miedo.	El cartero trajo **un paquete** para Marisol.	Yo quiero mucho a mis **padres**.	A la abuela le gustan **los parques**.
2021 paralyzed/paralysed*	2022 parcel	2023 parent	2024 park

El papá de Marisol siempre **estaciona** aquí.

2025   to park

la parka

2026   parka

En **el Parlamento** se hacen las leyes.

2027   parliament

Los loros son muy parlanchines.

2028   parrot

el perejil

2029   parsley

La pastinaca es una hortaliza europea.

2030   parsnip

En el aire siempre hay **partículas** de polvo.

2031   particle

Javier es buena **pareja** de baile.

2032   partner

A Marisol le encantan **las fiestas**.

2033   party

Pilar **pasó** la pelota tan mal. . .

2034   to pass

. . . que su hermano **se desmayó**.

2035   to pass out

el pasadizo

2036   passage

el pasajero

2037   passenger

Para sacar una visa hace falta **un pasaporte**.

2038   passport

el pasado

En **el pasado** no habían ni autos ni aviones.
El pretérito es el **pasado** de un verbo.

In the past, there were no planes or cars.
The preterit is a verb's past tense.

2039   past

Si comes muchos **fideos** te pones gordo.

2040   pasta

El papel mural se **empasta** con engrudo.

2041   to paste

El bordado es uno de **los pasatiempos** de mamá.

2042   pastime

¿A quién no le gustan **los pasteles**?

2043   pastry

Las ovejas pacen en **los pastizales**.

2044   pasture

Este **remiendo** lo puse yo mismo.

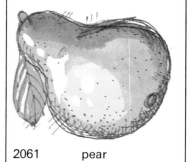

2045   patch

el sendero

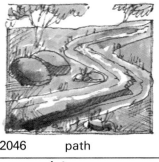

2046   path

Marisol es una niña muy **paciente**.

2047   She is patient.

un paciente asustado

2048   patient

el molde, el patrón para un vestido

2049   pattern

detenerse, hacer una pausa

Después de leer un par de páginas, Marisol se detuvo por unos segundos.
La partitura indica que el pianista hace una pausa.

After reading two pages, Marisol paused for a few seconds.
The score shows that the pianist must pause.

2050   to pause

caminar sobre **el pavimento**

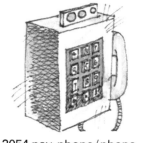

2051   pavement/road*

¿Cuántas **garras** tiene un gato?

2052   paw

Todo el mundo vive **pagando** cuentas.

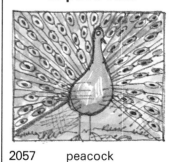

2053   to pay

el teléfono público

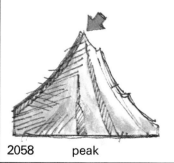

2054 pay phone/phone box*

paz en la tierra

2055   peace

el durazno, el melocotón

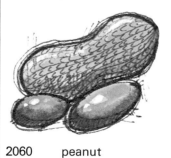

2056   peach

el pavo real

2057   peacock

la cima, la cumbre

2058   peak

Se oye **un repique** de campanas.

2059   peal of a bell

el maní, el cacahuete

2060   peanut

la pera

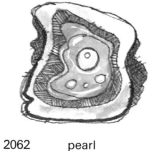

2061   pear

la perla

2062   pearl

las arvejas, los guisantes

2063   peas

La turba ayuda a las plantas a crecer.

2064   peat moss

Demóstenes se ponía **guijarros** en la boca.

2065   pebbles

La pacana es una nuez de norteamérica.

2066   pecan

picotear

2067   to peck

el pedal

2068   pedal

el peatón

2070   pedestrian

el cruce de peatones

2071   pedestrian crossing

pelar

2072   to peel

pedalear

2069   to pedal

el pelícano

2073   pelican

la pluma, el bolígrafo

2074   pen

el lápiz

2075   pencil

el reloj de **péndulo**

2076   pendulum

el pingüino, el pájaro bobo

2077   penguin

el cortaplumas

2078   penknife

El pentágono tiene cinco lados.

2079   pentagon

un grupo de **gente**

2080   people

el molinillo de **pimienta**

2081   pepper

la menta

2082   peppermint

la perca

2083   perch

El pajarillo posado en **la percha**.

2084   perch

una gran **actuación**

2085   performance

el perfume

2086   perfume

El punto se pone al final de una frase.

glurg!

2087   period/full stop*

la pervinca

2088   periwinkle

la persona

2089   person

la plaga

2090   pest

Mauricio **importuna** a su papá.

2091   to pester

una mascota fuera de lo común

2092   pet

Las flores tienen **pétalos**.

2094   petal

la petunia

2095   petunia

Los boticarios despachan recetas.

2096   pharmacist/chemist*

Al perrito le gusta que le **hagan cariño**.

2093   to pet

la farmacia, la botica

2097   pharmacy/chemist's*

el faisán

2098   pheasant

el teléfono

2099   phone

la fotografía

2100   photograph

el piano

2101   piano

Escoge una carta.

2102   to pick

Angélica **levanta** la muñeca.

2103   to pick up

el pico, el zapapico

2104   pickaxe

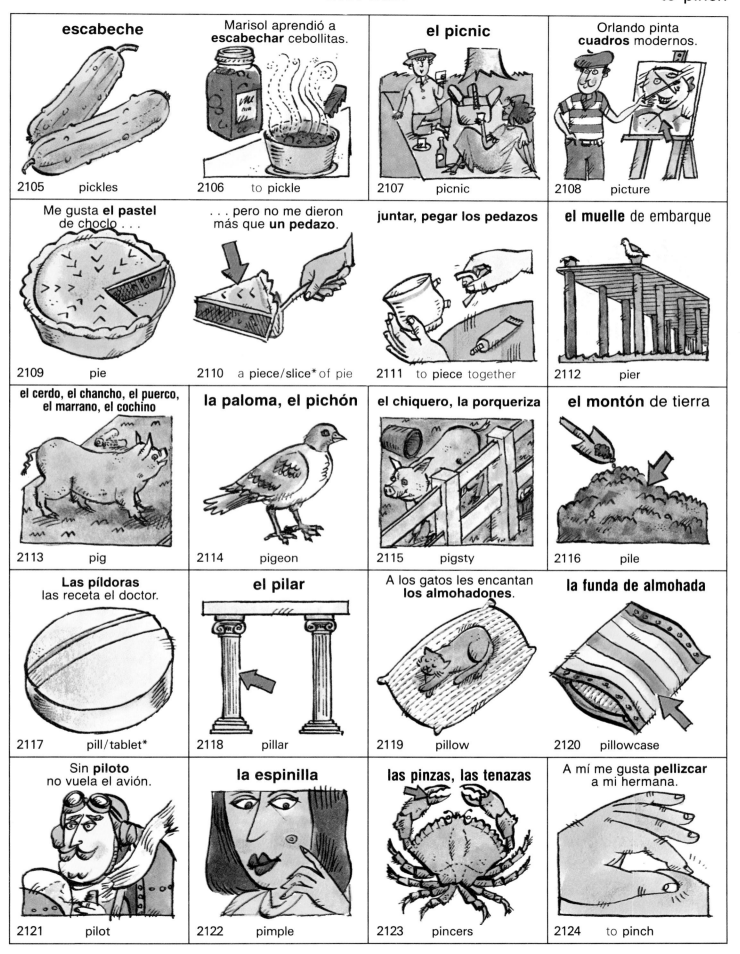

escabeche
2105 pickles

Marisol aprendió a **escabechar** cebollitas.
2106 to pickle

el picnic
2107 picnic

Orlando pinta **cuadros** modernos.
2108 picture

Me gusta **el pastel** de choclo . . .
2109 pie

. . . pero no me dieron más que **un pedazo**.
2110 a piece/slice* of pie

juntar, pegar los pedazos
2111 to piece together

el muelle de embarque
2112 pier

el cerdo, el chancho, el puerco, el marrano, el cochino
2113 pig

la paloma, el pichón
2114 pigeon

el chiquero, la porqueriza
2115 pigsty

el montón de tierra
2116 pile

Las píldoras las receta el doctor.
2117 pill/tablet*

el pilar
2118 pillar

A los gatos les encantan **los almohadones**.
2119 pillow

la funda de almohada
2120 pillowcase

Sin **piloto** no vuela el avión.
2121 pilot

la espinilla
2122 pimple

las pinzas, las tenazas
2123 pincers

A mí me gusta **pellizcar** a mi hermana.
2124 to pinch

el pino

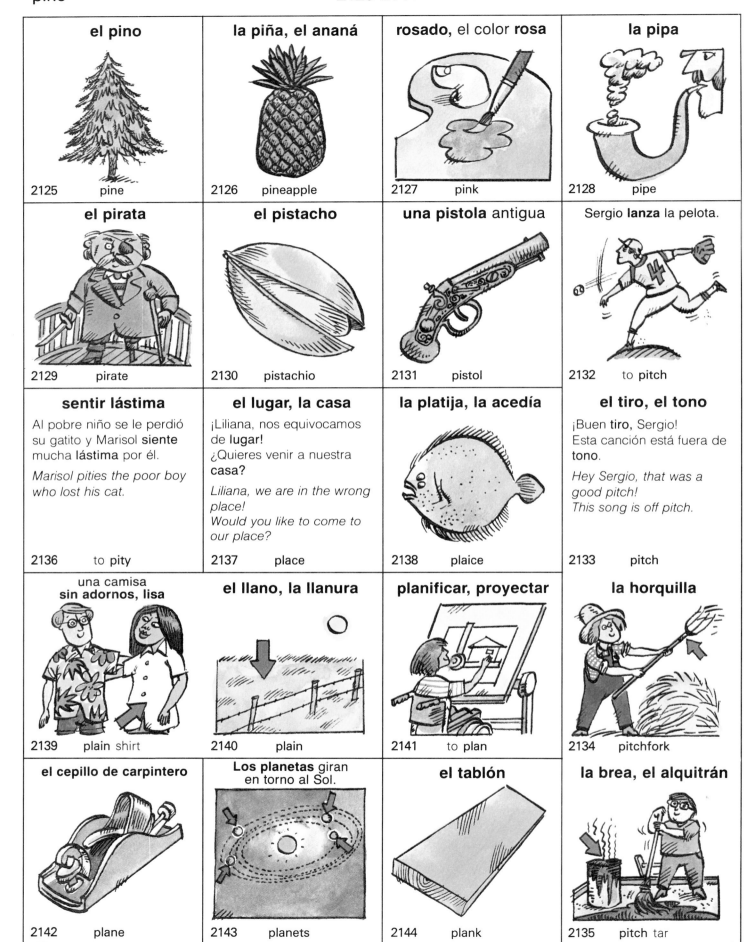

2125   pine

la piña, el ananá

2126   pineapple

rosado, el color **rosa**

2127   pink

la pipa

2128   pipe

el pirata

2129   pirate

el pistacho

2130   pistachio

una pistola antigua

2131   pistol

Sergio **lanza** la pelota.

2132   to pitch

sentir lástima

Al pobre niño se le perdió
su gatito y Marisol **siente**
mucha **lástima** por él.

*Marisol pities the poor boy
who lost his cat.*

2136   to pity

el lugar, la casa

¡Liliana, nos equivocamos
de **lugar**!
¿Quieres venir a nuestra
casa?

*Liliana, we are in the wrong
place!
Would you like to come to
our place?*

2137   place

la platija, la acedía

2138   plaice

el tiro, el tono

¡Buen **tiro**, Sergio!
Esta canción está fuera de
tono.

*Hey Sergio, that was a
good pitch!
This song is off pitch.*

2133   pitch

una camisa
sin adornos, lisa

2139   plain shirt

el llano, la llanura

2140   plain

planificar, proyectar

2141   to plan

la horquilla

2134   pitchfork

el cepillo de carpintero

2142   plane

Los planetas giran
en torno al Sol.

2143   planets

el tablón

2144   plank

la brea, el alquitrán

2135   pitch tar

las plantas	plantar	el yeso	Gabriela está **enluciendo** la pared con yeso.
2145 plants	2146 to plant	2147 plaster	2148 to plaster

el plástico	la plasticina	Marisol siempre come en su **plato** favorito.	la meseta, la altiplanicie
2149 plastic	2150 plasticine	2151 plate	2152 plateau

el **andén** del ferrocarril	jugar	el patio de juegos	el naipe, la carta
2153 platform	2154 to play	2155 playground	2156 playing cards

suplicar, implorar	un día muy **agradable**	Un vaso de leche, **por favor**.	La falda escocesa tiene muchos **pliegues**.
2157 to plead	2158 a pleasant day	2159 A glass of milk, **please**.	2160 pleat

los alicates	el arado	arrancar, desplumar	el enchufe
2161 pliers	2162 plow/plough*	2163 to pluck	2164 plug

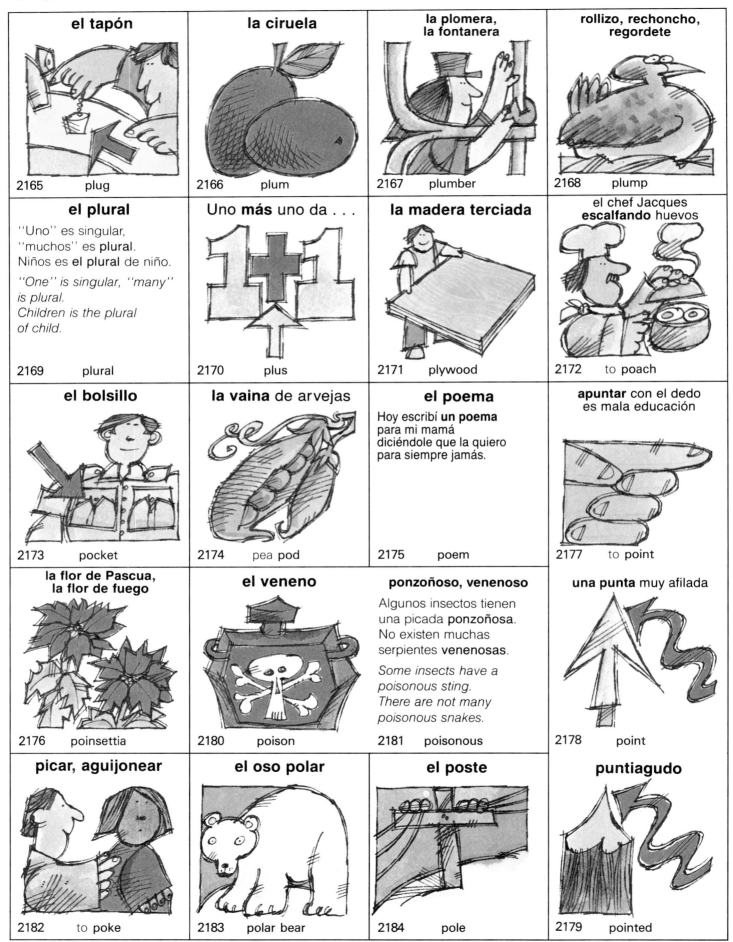

el tapón

2165 plug

la ciruela

2166 plum

la plomera, la fontanera

2167 plumber

rollizo, rechoncho, regordete

2168 plump

el plural

"Uno" es singular, "muchos" es **plural**. Niños es **el plural** de niño.

"One" is singular, "many" is plural. Children is the plural of child.

2169 plural

Uno más uno da . . .

2170 plus

la madera terciada

2171 plywood

el chef Jacques escalfando huevos

2172 to poach

el bolsillo

2173 pocket

la vaina de arvejas

2174 pea pod

el poema

Hoy escribí **un poema** para mi mamá diciéndole que la quiero para siempre jamás.

2175 poem

apuntar con el dedo es mala educación

2177 to point

la flor de Pascua, la flor de fuego

2176 poinsettia

el veneno

2180 poison

ponzoñoso, venenoso

Algunos insectos tienen una picada **ponzoñosa**. No existen muchas serpientes **venenosas**.

Some insects have a poisonous sting. There are not many poisonous snakes.

2181 poisonous

una punta muy afilada

2178 point

picar, aguijonear

2182 to poke

el oso polar

2183 polar bear

el poste

2184 pole

puntiagudo

2179 pointed

el policía

2185   policeman

la mujer policía

2186   policewoman

pulir, bruñir, lustrar

2187   to polish

atento, bien educado, cortés

Martín es muy **atento**.
Las personas **bien educadas** ceden su asiento en el bus.
Hernán Cortés no era muy **cortés**.

Martin is a very polite child.
Polite people give up their seat on the bus.
Hernan Cortes was not very polite.

2188   polite

el polen

2189   pollen

la granada

2190   pomegranate

el estanque

2191   pond

el caballito, el poni

2192   pony

la piscina, la pileta, la alberca

2193   pool

Los vecinos **aunaron** sus esfuerzos.

2194   to pool

deficiente, pobre

Marisol tuvo notas muy **deficientes** este semestre.
Pobre diablo, se le perdió su cachimba.

Marisol had very poor marks this term.
Poor devil, he lost his pipe.

2195   poor

saltar, reventar, estallar

2196   to pop

el álamo

2197   poplar

la amapola

2198   poppy

popular

A Marisol no le gusta la música **popular**.
Este es un libro muy **popular**.

Marisol dislikes popular music.
This book is very popular.

2199   popular

Memo sale al **porche** por las tardes.

2200   porch

Los poros son agujeritos que tenemos en la piel.

2201   Pores are little holes in the skin.

avena cocida con leche

2202   porridge

el puerto

2203   port

portátil

Marisol está juntando su mesada para comprar una radio **portátil**.

Marisol wants a portable radio but she has not saved up enough money from her allowance.

2204   portable

el botones, el mozo de cuerda, el cargador

2205 porter

Este es **un retrato** de la Tía Adriana.

2206 portrait

---

el poste

2207 post

Orlando **despachó** una carta.

2208 to post

---

la tarjeta postal

2210 postcard

---

el cartel

2211 poster

---

la olla

2212 pot

---

la oficina de correos

2209 post office

---

la papa, la patata

2213 potato

---

los cacharros, la alfarería

2214 pottery

---

la bolsa, el saquito

2215 pouch

---

abalanzarse

2216 to pounce

---

la perrera, la libra

Los perros vagabundos van a parar a **la perrera**.
Cuatro plátanos pesan cerca de **una libra**.
La libra esterlina es la moneda de Inglaterra.

Stray dogs are taken to the dog pound.
Four bananas weigh about a pound.
The pound sterling is Britain's currency.

2217 pound

---

golpear, triturar, machacar

2218 to pound

---

verter, escanciar, vaciar, echar

2219 to pour

---

enfurruñarse, hacer pucheros

2220 to pout

---

los polvos talco

2221 powder

---

ensayar, practicar

2222 to practice/practise*

En **las praderas** se cultiva el trigo.

2223 prairie

---

elogiar, alabar

2224 to praise

Los caballos **corvetean**.

2225   to prance

rezar, orar

2226   to pray

Yo **prefiero** éste.

2227   to prefer

Esta señora está **embarazada**.

2228   She is pregnant.

¿González? ¡**Presente**, señor!

2229   I am present.

el obsequio, el regalo de cumpleaños

2230   birthday present

Tomás **hace entrega** del trofeo.

2231   to present

frutas en **conserva**

2232   preserved fruit

Aprieta el botón.

2233   to press

linda, bonita

2234   pretty

el búho y su **presa**

2235   prey

el precio

2236   price

pinchar, pincharse

2237   to prick

el bicho **espinudo**

2238   prickly animal

la escuela primaria

2239   primary school

la primavera

2240   primrose

el príncipe

2241   prince

la princesa

2242   princess

la directora de mi escuela

2243   school principal/Head teacher*

el principio

En **principio** estaría de acuerdo contigo.
La honestidad es una cuestión de **principios**.
Decir la verdad es un **principio** fundamental.

In principle, I agree with you.
Honesty is a matter of principle.
Truth is a sacred principle.

2244   principle

imprimir	La luz se descompone cuando pasa por **un prisma**.	Malandrín terminó en **prisión** por sus bellaquerías.	**el preso, el prisionero**
2245 to print	2246 prism	2247 prison	2248 prisoner

privado, particular, reservado

Marisol y yo tuvimos una conversación **privada**.
Martín toma clases **particulares**.
Él es una persona muy **reservada**.

Marisol and I are having a private talk.
Martin takes private lessons.
He is a very private person.

2249   private

Iris ganó el primer **premio** en el campeonato de natación.

2250   prize

el problema

2251   problem

frutas y verduras

2252   produce

La televisión pasa **programas** bastante mediocres.

2254   program/programme*

se prohibe, prohibido

2255   prohibited

el proyecto

Ximena está ocupada con **un proyecto**.
A Marisol le fue mal con su **proyecto**.

Ximena is working on a project.
Marisol did not do well on her project.

2256   project

Esta fábrica **produce** automóviles.

2253   This factory **produces** cars.

yo prometo, me comprometo

2257   I promise.

una horquilla de cuatro **puntas**

2258   prong

Cuando hables, **pronuncia** con claridad.

2259   to pronounce

Aquí está **la prueba** de que Micifuz se comió el canario.

2260   proof of guilt

apuntalar, sostener

2261   to prop

la hélice

2262   propeller

Ponte **bien** la ropa.

2263   properly dressed

la propiedad

Cuando Marisol dice "esto es mío", quiere decir "esto es de mi **propiedad**".
Su familia tiene **propiedades** en el campo.

Marisol says "This is mine" when she means "This is my property".
Her family owns property in the country.

2264   property

protestar

2265   to protest

un gato orgulloso

2266   I am a proud cat.

Usía, yo voy a demostrar que es así.

2267   to prove

el proverbio

Un antiguo **proverbio** chino:
''Cuando el río suena, es porque se cayó un piano al agua.''

Here is a proverb:
''An apple a day keeps the doctor away.''

2268   proverb

La escuela nos ha proporcionado sillas.

2269   to provide chairs

la ciruela pasa

2270   prune

podar

2271   to prune

el teléfono público

2272   public telephone/phone box*

Tenemos budín de postre.

2273   pudding/afters*

el charco, la poza

2274   puddle

dar bocanadas, resoplar

2275   to puff

el frailecillo

2276   puffin

tirar, jalar, halar

2277   to pull

la polea, la roldana

2278   pulley

el pulóver, el suéter

2279   pullover/sweater*

El doctor me tomó el pulso.

2280   pulse

la bomba de agua

2281   pump

bombear

2282   to pump

el zapallo, la calabaza

2283   pumpkin

dar puñetazos

2284   to punch

Eres muy **puntual**.

2285   You are punctual.

Pinchar un neumático no es ninguna gracia.

2286   to puncture

castigar

2287   to punish

el castigo

2288   punishment

Pinocho es **un títere** de madera.

2289   puppet

el cachorro

2290   puppy

Ya no quedan muchos manantiales de agua **pura**.

2291   pure water

morado, púrpura

2292   purple

Los gatos **ronronean** cuando están contentos.

2293   to purr

el bolso, la cartera

2294   purse/handbag*

perseguir

2295   to pursue

empujar

2296   to push

Ponlo por aquí, por favor.

2297   to put

guardar

2298   to put away

Postergar los deberes no es buen método.

2299   to put off

La masilla afirma los vidrios.

2300   putty

el rompecabezas

2301   puzzle

el pijama, el piyama

2302   pyjamas*/pajamas

la pirámide

2303   pyramid

la serpiente **pitón**

2304   python

la codorniz

2305   quail

un reloj de **calidad**

2306   quality watch

una taza para medir **cantidades**

2307   quantity

pelear, reñir

2308   to quarrel

El mármol y la piedra salen de **las canteras.**

2309   quarry

un cuarto

1/4

2310   quarter

Un bote llegó al **embarcadero.**

2311   quay

la reina

2312   queen

hacer **una pregunta**

2313   to ask a question

¡Vuelve **rápido**!

2314   quick

Las arenas movedizas son muy peligrosas.

2315   quicksand

Ella es muy **tranquila.**

2316   She is quiet.

La pluma es más fuerte que la espada.

2317   quill

Los puercoespines tienen **púas.**

2318   porcupine quill

la colcha

2319   quilt/eiderdown*

Los niños llevan **membrillos** al colegio.

2320   quince

El carcaj sirve para llevar las flechas.

2321   quiver

temblar, estremecerse

2322   to quiver

la prueba

Hoy tuvimos **prueba** de ortografía en la escuela.

Our class had a quiz in spelling today.

2323   quiz

R

el conejo
2324   rabbit

el mapache, el oso lavador
2325   raccoon

echar carrera
2326   to race

la percha
2327   rack/hat-stand*

el alboroto, la baraúnda
2328   racket

el radiador
2329   radiator

la radio
2330   radio

los rábanos
2331   radish

¿Sabes sacar **el radio** del círculo?
2332   radius

la balsa
2333   raft

una **invasión** de hormigas
2334   a **raid** in progress

La baranda sirve para afirmarse.
2335   handrail/banister*

la vía férrea
2336   railroad track/railway track*

¡Está **lloviendo** a chuzos!
2337   to rain

A todos los niños les gustan **los arco iris**.
2338   rainbow

el impermeable
2339   raincoat

levantar, plantear

¡Todos los que quieren a Marisol, que **levanten** la mano!
La pregunta que ella **plantea** es bastante interesante.

All those who like Marisol, raise your hands!
She has raised an interesting question.

2340   to raise

Las pasas son uvas secas.
2341   raisin

el rastrillo
2342   rake

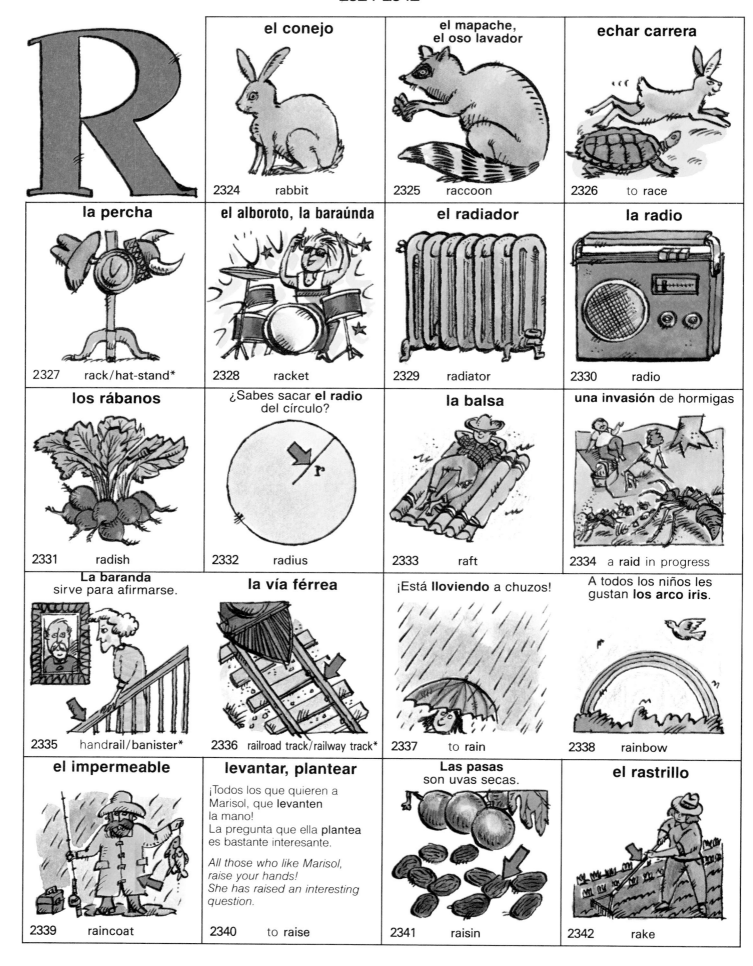

El cartero **golpea** dos veces.

2343　　to rap/knock*

rápido, veloz, raudo

2344　　rapid

raro, excepcional

2345　　rare

el sarpullido

2346　　rash

las frambuesas

2347　　raspberry

la rata

2348　　rat

el cascabel, el sonajero

2349　　rattle

la serpiente cascabel

2350　　rattlesnake

el cuervo

2351　　raven

famélico, voraz

2352　　ravenous

el barranco, la hondonada

2353　　ravine

un huevo **crudo**

2354　　a raw egg

el rayo de luz

2355　　ray of sunlight

la navaja de afeitar

2356　　razor

alcanzar

2357　　to reach

leer

2358　　to read

Prepararse . . . **listo** . . .¡Ya!

2359　　ready

¿Será **verdadero** este diamante?

2360　　real

darse cuenta

2361　　to realize/realise*

¿De veras que has llegado?

2362　　Are you **really** here?

el trasero

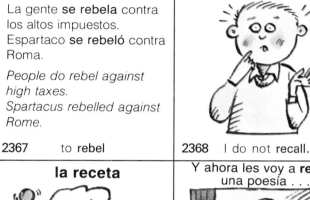

2363   rear

el retrovisor

2364   rearview mirror

razonar, discutir, argüir

2365   to reason

módico, razonable

Este es un precio bastante **módico**.
¡Marisol, por favor, sé más **razonable**!

That is a reasonable price.
Marisol, please be reasonable.

2366   reasonable

rebelarse

La gente **se rebela** contra los altos impuestos.
Espartaco **se rebeló** contra Roma.

People do rebel against high taxes.
Spartacus rebelled against Rome.

2367   to rebel

No me puedo **acordar**.

2368   I do not **recall**.

recibir

2369   to receive

un pollito **recién** nacido

2370   recently hatched

la receta

2371   recipe

Y ahora les voy a **recitar** una poesía . . .

2372   to recite

el disco   el tocadiscos

2373   record   2374   record player

recuperarse, recobrar

Marisol se raspó la rodilla pero ya **se recuperó**.
Logré **recobrar** todos los libros que se quedaron afuera.

Marisol scraped her knee but she's already recovered.
I recovered all the books that were left outside.

2375   to recover

el rectángulo

2376   rectangle

el color **rojo**

2377   red

la caña, el junco

2378   reed

el **arrecife** de coral

2379   reef

¡Esa alcantarilla **apesta**!

2380   to reek

Las cañas de pescar tienen **un carrete**.

2381   reel

el árbitro

2382   referee

Las imágenes de un espejo se llaman reflejos.

2383   reflection

Siempre deja bien cerrado el refrigerador.

2384   refrigerator

rechazar, rehusar

2385   to refuse

una región

2386   region

inscribir, inscribirse

2387   to register

El pobre Martín lamenta mucho lo que pasó.

2388   to regret

Los actores ensayan una obra.

2389   Actors rehearse a play.

el reno

2390   reindeer

las riendas

2391   reins

los parientes, los familiares

2392   relatives

descansar, reposar

2393   to relax

soltar, liberar, poner en libertad

2394   to release

Acuérdate de lavarte los dientes.

2395   Remember to brush your teeth.

una isla muy remota

2396   remote island

quitar, sacar

2397   to remove

alquilar, arrendar

Nosotros **alquilamos** un departamento.
Si no tienes auto, podrías **arrendar** uno.

We rent an apartment.
If you do not have a car, you can rent one.

2398   to rent

arreglar, reparar

2399   to repair

Los loros repiten lo que tú les digas.

2400   to repeat

cambiar, reponer

2401   to replace

¿Me podrías responder una pregunta?

2402   to reply

el reptil

2403   reptile

Javier **rescató** al pobre gatito.

2404   to rescue

---

el tanque, el depósito

2405   reservoir

---

responsable

Marisol, tú eres **responsable** de tu hermanito Raúl.
Papá vio la leche derramada en el suelo y dijo: ''¿Quién es el **responsable** de esto?''

Marisol, you are responsible for your little brother Raul.
Dad saw the milk spilled on the floor and said: "Who is responsible for this?"

2406   responsible

---

descansar

2407   to rest

---

el restaurante, el restorán

2408   restaurant

---

devolver, volver

Marisol siempre **devuelve** los libros que saca de la biblioteca.
Gabriel anda de viaje pero **volverá** pronto.

Marisol always returns her library books.
Gabriel is travelling but he will return soon.

2409   to return

---

la marcha atrás

2410   reverse

---

el rinoceronte

2411   rhinoceros

---

el ruibarbo

2412   rhubarb

---

la rima

Este es un verso con **rima**:
Soy chiquitito
como una pepita de ají
pero tengo el corazón grande
para quererte a ti.

2413   rhyme

¿Será ésta **la costilla** de Adán?

2414   rib

---

un paquete adornado con **cinta** para regalo

2415   ribbon

El arroz es muy rico y nutritivo.

2416   rice

---

intenso, rico

Este género es de un rojo **intenso**.
Ese es un colegio para **ricos**.

The fabric is a rich red color.
That's a school for the rich.

2417   rich

¡Vaya qué **misterio**!

2418   riddle

---

montar, cabalgar

2419   to **ride** a horse

---

el cerro, el reborde

2420   ridge

Esta es mi mano **derecha**.

2421   my **right** hand

---

la derecha, bien, cierto

Al llegar a la esquina dobla a **la derecha**.
No está **bien** robar.
Marisol cree que siempre está en lo **cierto**.

Turn right at the corner.
It is not right to steal.
Marisol thinks she is always right.

2422   right

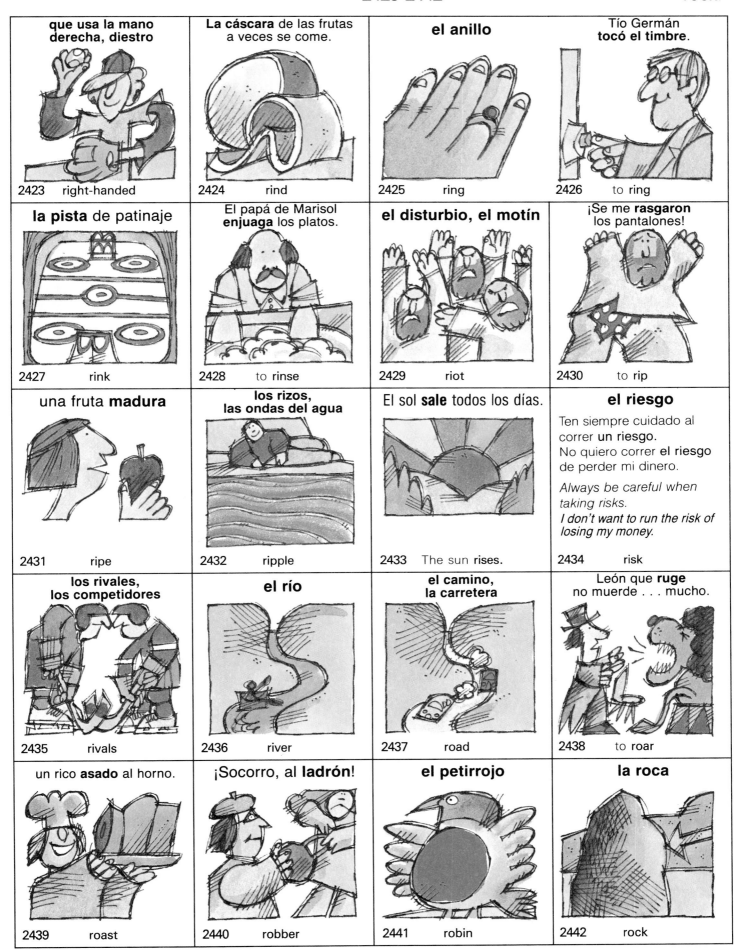

que usa la mano derecha, diestro

2423   right-handed

La cáscara de las frutas a veces se come.

2424   rind

el anillo

2425   ring

Tío Germán **tocó el timbre**.

2426   to ring

la pista de patinaje

2427   rink

El papá de Marisol **enjuaga** los platos.

2428   to rinse

el disturbio, el motín

2429   riot

¡Se me **rasgaron** los pantalones!

2430   to rip

una fruta **madura**

2431   ripe

los rizos, las ondas del agua

2432   ripple

El sol **sale** todos los días.

Ten siempre cuidado al correr **un riesgo**.
No quiero correr **el riesgo** de perder mi dinero.

Always be careful when taking risks.
I don't want to run the risk of losing my money.

2433   The sun **rises**.

el riesgo

2434   risk

los rivales, los competidores

2435   rivals

el río

2436   river

el camino, la carretera

2437   road

León que **ruge** no muerde . . . mucho.

2438   to roar

un rico **asado** al horno.

2439   roast

¡Socorro, al **ladrón**!

2440   robber

el petirrojo

2441   robin

la roca

2442   rock

balancearse, mecerse	el cohete	la mecedora	la caña de pescar
2443 to rock	2444 rocket	2445 rocking chair	2446 rod
el rollo de papel	rodar	los patines de ruedas	el uslero, el rodillo
2447 roll	2448 to roll	2449 roller skate	2450 rolling pin
el techo de la casa	el cuarto, la sala, la habitación	descansar las aves en una percha	la raíz
2451 roof	2452 room	2453 to roost	2454 root
la soga, la cuerda	la rosa	el romero	María Paz tiene las mejillas rosadas.
2455 rope	2456 rose	2457 rosemary	2458 rosy
una manzana podrida	una barba áspera	redondo	cuatro botones en fila
2459 rotten apple	2460 rough	2461 round	2462 4 buttons in a row

Lucía **rema** más rápido que su hermano.

2463   to row

El rey es el jefe de la casa **real**.

2464   royal

Los neumáticos y las pelotas se hacen de **caucho**.

2465   rubber

la basura, los desechos

2466   rubbish

el rubí

2467   ruby

el timón

2468   rudder

un tipo **grosero**

2469   He is rude.

un territorio **escarpado, escabroso**

2470   rugged terrain

Estas son **las ruinas** de un antiguo castillo.

2471   ruin

la regla

La excepción confirma la regla.
Tú conoces **las reglas** del juego.

The exception confirms the rule.
You know the rules of the game.

2472   rule

Este es **un gobernante** antiguo.

2473   ruler

Se oye **el retumbo** de un tren.

2474   I hear a rumble.

Nunca **corras** al cruzar la calle.

2475   to run

huir, escaparse

2476   to run away

atropellar

2477   to run over

agotarse

2478   to run out of energy

apurarse, apresurarse, darse prisa

2479   to rush

el óxido

2480   rust

el bache, la rodada

2481   rut

Me gusta el pan **centeno**.

2482   rye

el saco de harina

2483   sack

Decir la verdad es un precepto **sagrado**.

2484   Truth is a **sacred** principle.

triste

2485   sad

la montura

2486   saddle

¿Qué hay en **la caja fuerte**?

2487   safe

la vela de una carabela

2488   sail

la tabla, la plancha a vela

2489   sailboard

el velero

2490   sailboat/sailing boat*

el marino, el marinero

2491   sailor

la ensalada

2492   salad

a precios de **liquidación**

2493   sale

el salmón

2494   salmon

la sal y la pimienta

2495   salt

saludar, hacer un saludo

2496   to salute

igual, lo **mismo**

2497   same

un reloj de **arena**

2498   sand

la sandalia

2499   sandal

De almuerzo me comí **un sandwich**.

2500   sandwich

la savia

2501   sap

como sardinas en lata	**el satélite**	un vestido de **raso**	**el sábado**
2502 sardine	2503 satellite	2504 satin dress	**El sábado** es el sexto día de la semana. **Los sábados** se juega y nada más. A Marisol le encantan los **sábados.** *Saturday is the sixth day of the week.* *Saturday is play day.* *Marisol likes Saturdays.* 2505 Saturday
la salsa	**la salchicha**	Yo **ahorro** dinero.	**El serrucho** es una herramienta muy útil.
2506 sauce/gravy*	2507 sausage	2508 I save my money.	2509 saw
Aserrín, aserrán, los maderos de San Juan . . .	Yo **digo** las cosas tal como son.	**el andamiaje**	**aserruchar, aserrar, serrar**
2511 sawdust	2512 I say what I think.	2513 scaffolding	2510 to saw
quemarse con agua hirviendo, escaldarse	El fiel de **la balanza** controla el peso.	**¡Los ostiones** son cosa muy rica, señor!	**el cuero cabelludo**
2514 to scald	2515 scale	2516 scallop	2517 scalp
una cicatriz en la cara y otra en el corazón	A Martín le revienta que lo **asusten.**	**Los espantapájaros** no tienen cerebro.	**la bufanda**
2518 scar	2519 to scare	2520 scarecrow	2521 scarf

el color **escarlata**

2522   scarlet

El criminal vuelve a **la escena** del crimen.

2523   scene of a crime

el paisaje

2524   scenery

El saber no ocupa lugar.

2525   scholarship

Esta es **la escuela** de Marisol.

2526   school

la goleta

2527   schooner

las tijeras

2528   scissors

sacar con cuchara o pala

2529   to scoop

la motoneta

2530   scooter

un papel **chamuscado**

2531 scorched paper

marcar un tanto, meter un gol

2532   to score

un niño explorador

2533   scout

unos pedazos de papel

2534 scraps of paper

¡Otra **raspadura**!

2535   scrape

el raspador

2536   scraper

el rasguño

2537   scratch

la rejilla

2538   screen

el tornillo

2539   screw

el atornillador, el destornillador

2540   screwdriver

Mamá trabaja **fregando** pisos.

2541   to scrub

el escultor

2542   sculptor

**el caballito de mar,
el hipocampo**

2543   seahorse

El Mar Adriático está
cerca del **Mar** Jónico.

2544   Adriatic sea

la gaviota

2545   seagull

la foca

2546   seal

una costura

2547   seam

buscar, explorar

2548   to search

el reflector

2549   searchlight

la estación

Las cuatro **estaciones** son:
primavera verano otoño
invierno

*The four seasons are:
Spring Summer Autumn
Winter*

2550   seasons

el asiento

2551   seat

Marisol siempre se pone **el
cinturón de seguridad**.

2552   seatbelt

las algas

2553   seaweed

Llegó **segundo**.

2554   second

Tengo **un secreto**.

2555   I have a secret.

ver

2556   to see

**el balancín,
el sube y baja**

2557   see-saw

la semilla

2558   seed

Parece que se murió . . .

2559   It seems to be dead.

agarrar, coger

2560   to seize

A nadie le gustan las
personas **egoístas**.

2561   You are selfish.

Iris vende frutas.

2562   to sell

el semicírculo

2563   semicircle

enviar, despachar, remitir

2564   to send

La tarde al sol me dejó la piel **sensible.**

2565   sensitive skin

la frase, la sentencia

¿Tú podrías escribir una frase?
Al ladrón le dieron una larga sentencia.

Can you make a sentence?
The robber received a long prison sentence.

2566   sentence

el centinela

2567   sentry

Septiembre es el noveno mes del año.

2568   September

servir

2569   to serve

el número **siete**

2570   seven

séptimo

2571   seventh

varios

2572   several

coser y cantar

2573   to sew

la máquina de coser

2574   sewing machine

andrajoso, harapiento

2575   shabby

la choza

2576   shack

la sombra

2577   shadow

un perro **lanudo**

2578   shaggy

sacudir, agitar

2579   to shake

agua **poco profunda**

2580   shallow water

Mamá se lava el pelo con **champú.**

2581   shampoo

Yo **comparto** lo que tengo con los demás.

2582　　to share

Los tiburones no tienen huesos en el cuerpo.

2583　　shark

afilado

2584　　sharp

el afilador de cuchillos

2585　　knife sharpener

El vaso **se hizo añicos**.

2588　　to shatter

afeitar, rasurarse

2589　　to shave

las cizallas, las tijeras de podar

2590　　shears

el afilador de patines

2586　　skate sharpener

la funda

2591　　sheath

Marisol cuenta **ovejas** para quedarse dormida.

2592　　sheep

la sábana

2593　　sheet

el sacapuntas

2587　　pencil sharpener

el estante, la repisa

2594　　shelf

la concha

2595　　shell

a buen **resguardo**

2596　　shelter

el pastor

2597　　shepherd

el escudo

2598　　shield

la canilla

2599　　shin

El sol **brilla** esplendoroso.

2600　　to shine

Los tejados tienen **tejas.**

2601　　shingle

La zona es una enfermedad cutánea.

2602 shingles

brillante, resplandeciente

2603 shiny

la embarcación, la nave

2604 ship

el naufragio

2605 shipwreck

la camisa

2606 shirt

tiritar, temblar

2607 to shiver

¡Cuidado con **los golpes eléctricos!**

2608 shock

los zapatos

2609 shoes

los cordones, los pasadores

2610 shoelace

el zapatero

2611 shoemaker

disparar, tirar

2612 to shoot

la tienda, el almacén

2613 shop

el almacenero, el tendero

2614 shopkeeper

la vitrina, el escaparate

2615 shop window

a **orillas** del mar

2616 shore

bajo

2617 short

los pantalones cortos, los shorts

2618 shorts

el hombro

2619 shoulder

gritar

2620 to shout

Empujar a alguien es pésima educación.

2621 to shove

la pala	**mostrar, enseñar**	**alardear, vanagloriarse, hacer ostentación**	**Por fin apareció.**
2622 shovel	2623 to show	2624 to show off	2625 to show up/appear*
Ricardo canta en **la ducha**.	**chillar, dar alaridos**	**el camarón, la gamba**	**encoger, encogerse**
2626 shower	2627 to shriek	2628 shrimp	2629 to shrink
el arbusto	Así se **baraja** la baraja.	**los postigos, las contraventanas**	**tímido, vergonzoso**
2630 shrub	2631 shuffle	2632 shutters	2633 shy
enfermo	**el lado, el costado**	Siempre es mejor caminar por **la vereda**.	al salir del examen **suspiré** de alivio
2634 sick	2635 side	2636 sidewalk/pavement*	2637 to sigh
el letrero, el cartel	**indicar, señalar**	mi **firma**	**callado, silencioso**
2638 sign	2639 to signal	2640 signature	2641 silent

Marisol nunca se está **callada** mucho rato.
Una noche **silenciosa** es una noche tranquila.

Marisol is not silent very often.
A silent night is a quiet night.

el pretil de la ventana	**tonto, necio**	**la plata**	**simple, sencillo**
	Manolito dice que Marisol es **tonta**. Marisol piensa que el **necio** es Manolito. *Manolito thinks Marisol is silly.* *Marisol thinks Manolito is the silly one.*		Esa es la pura y **simple** verdad. Esto tiene una solución muy **sencilla**. *That is the truth, pure and simple.* *There is a simple solution.*
2642 sill	2643 silly	2644 silver	2645 simple
cantar	**singular** Plural es lo contrario de **singular**. "Uno" es **singular**. *Plural is the opposite of singular.* *"One is singular.*	**el lavatorio, el lavamanos, el lavabo**	**¡Nos hundimos!**
2646 to sing	2647 singular	2648 sink	2649 to sink
Alejandra **sorbe** su trago con fruición.	Esta **sirena** no sabe nadar.	Esta es mi **hermana** Lili.	**tomar asiento, sentarse**
2650 to sip	2651 siren	2652 sister	2653 to sit
seis	**sexto**	**¿Será de mi talla?**	**patinar**
2654 six	2655 sixth	2656 size	2657 to skate
el monopatín	**¡Ojalá tuviéramos un esqueleto de repuesto!**	**hacer un boceto, un croquis, un bosquejo**	**los esquíes**
2658 skateboard	2659 skeleton	2660 to sketch	2661 skis

esquiar

2662   to ski

resbalarse, patinar

2663   to skid

la piel

2664   skin

saltar la cuerda

2665   to skip

**el capitán,
el patrón del barco**

2666   skipper/captain*

la falda

2667   skirt

el cráneo, una calavera

2668   skull

el cielo

2669   sky

la alondra, la calandria

2670   skylark

Un rascacielos es un edificio muy alto.

2671   skyscraper

Raúl **cerró de un portazo**.

2672   to slam

un piso **inclinado**

2673   slanting floor

**abofetear,
dar una palmada**

2674   to slap

El Zorro **da tajos** a destajo.

2675   to slash

la pizarra

2676   slate

el trineo

2677   sled/sleigh*

De día, Zorro **duerme**.

2678   to sleep

el saco de dormir

2679   sleeping bag

Jorge **tiene sueño**.

2680   sleepy

la cellisca

2681   sleet

la manga 2682 sleeve	**el resbalín, el tobogán** 2683 slide	**delgada, flaca** 2684 slim	**un bicho viscoso** 2685 slimy
con el brazo en **cabestrillo** 2686 sling	**la honda, el tirador** 2687 slingshot/catapult*	**resbalar, resbalarse** 2688 to slip	**la zapatilla, la pantufla** 2689 slipper
resbaloso 2690 slippery	un tipo **mugriento** y **ordinario** 2691 slob	**la ladera** 2692 slope	**la ranura** 2693 slot
No **andes** tan **desgarbado.** 2694 to slouch	**disminuir la velocidad, ir más despacio, parar** El auto **disminuyó la velocidad** al llegar a la esquina. **¡Más despacio,** papá! Estás yendo muy rápido. A Marisol no la **para** nadie. *The car slows down at the corner. Slow down, Dad! You are going too fast. Nothing can slow down Marisol.* 2695 to slow down	**el aguanieve** 2696 slush	**pequeño** 2697 small
listo, sensato, elegante Marisol se cree muy **lista** porque le fue bien en el examen. Lo que hiciste fue muy **sensato.** El vestido que lleva es muy **elegante.** *Marisol thinks she is very smart because she passed her exam. That was a smart thing to do. She is wearing a smart dress.* 2698 smart/clever*	**¡No hagas pedazos** el reloj! 2699 to smash	**manchar, embadurnar, hacer un borrón** 2700 to smear	A Luis le gusta **oler** las flores. 2701 to smell

¡Qué zorrillo más hediondo!

2702   smelly

Los que fuman son como zorrillos.

2703   to smoke

suave, parejo

La seda es una tela muy **suave**.
Este camino es muy **parejo**.

Silk is a very smooth fabric.
This is a very smooth road.

2704   smooth

comerse un tentempié

2705   to have a snack

Caracol, caracol, saca tus cachitos al sol.

2706   snail

una culebra, una serpiente

2707   snake

partirse en dos, romperse

2708   to snap

las zapatillas

2709   sneakers/trainers*

estornudar

2710   to sneeze

el tubo respiratorio, el snorkel

2711   snorkel

la nieve

2712   snow

el copo de nieve

2713   snowflake

las raquetas de nieve

2714   snowshoes

Lávate con agua y **jabón**.

2715   soap

el fútbol, pasión de multitudes

2716   soccer

el calcetín

2717   sock

el enchufe, el tomacorriente

2718   socket

el sofá

2719   sofa/couch*

Suave será, pero igual araña.

2720   soft

el soldado

2721   soldier

Los lenguados son muy deslenguados.

2722   sole

Resolvió el problema.

2723   She **solves** the problem.

dar un salto mortal

2724   to **somersault**

Este es mi **hijo**.

2725   son

el canto, la canción

2726   song

dentro de poco, luego, al poco rato

Va a oscurecer **dentro de poco**.
Marisol vuelve **luego**.
Al poco rato se cansó de la muñeca nueva.

Soon it will be dark.
Marisol will be home soon.
She soon tired of her new doll.

2727   soon

el hechicero, el brujo

2728   sorcerer

Tengo el brazo **adolorido**.

2729   My arm is **sore**.

La acedera es muy sabrosa.

2730   sorrel

Macabeo está muy **arrepentido** de lo que hizo.

2731   sorry

separar, escoger, seleccionar

2732   to **sort**

¿Qué odiaba Mafalda? **¡La sopa!**

2733   soup

agrio, ácido

2734   sour

rumbo al **sur**

2735   south

una cerda, chancha, puerca, marrana, cochina

2736   sow

sembrar

2737   to **sow**

la nave espacial

2738   spaceship

la pala

2739   spade

zurrar

2740   to **spank**

Siempre conviene tener un neumático de **repuesto**.

2741   spare tire/tyre*

la chispa	Los anillos **relumbran** a la luz.	**el gorrión**	¿Cuántos idiomas sabes **hablar**?
2742　　spark	2743　　to sparkle	2744　　sparrow	2745　　to speak
una lanza	La tortuga va a paso de tortuga incluso cuando **acelera**.	**deletrear**	**gastar**
2746　　spear	2747　　to speed up	2748　　to spell	2749　　to spend
Las esferas son redondas.	**picante** y **condimentado**	**Las arañas** no arañan.	**la punta, la púa**
2750　　sphere	2751　　spicy	2752　　spider	2753　　spike
derramar, desparramar	**girar, dar vueltas**	**la espinaca**	**la espina dorsal**
2754　　to spill	2755　　to spin	2756　　spinach	2757　　spine
la espiral	**la aguja** de una iglesia	Las personas bien educadas no **escupen**.	**salpicar**
2758　　spiral	2759　　spire	2760　　to spit	2761　　to splash

Saltan **astillas** por todos lados.
2762 splinter

la fruta **podrida**
2763 spoiled/rotten* fruit

la esponja
2764 sponge

el carrete o **la bobina** de hilo
2765 spool/reel*

la cuchara
2766 spoon

¿Y de dónde salió esta **mancha**?
2767 spot

el pico de la tetera
2768 spout

Marisol **se torció** un tobillo.
2769 to sprain

rociar
2770 to spray

esparcir
2771 to spread

el resorte, el muelle
2772 spring

¡Al fin llegó **la primavera**!
2773 spring

espolvorear
2775 to sprinkle

correr a gran velocidad
2776 to sprint

el abeto
2777 spruce

El manantial trae agua fría y fresca.
2774 spring

un cuadrado
2778 square

la calabaza, el calabacín
2779 squash

ponerse en cuclillas
2780 to squat

Marisol **estrechó** a Rosita en sus brazos.
2781 to squeeze

el calamar

2782   squid

la ardilla

2783   squirrel

chorrear, salir a chorros

2784   to squirt

Los caballos viven en **los establos**.

2785   stable

el escenario del teatro

2786   stage

la mancha

2787   stain

la escalera

2788   staircase

una estaca de madera

2789   wooden stake

añejo

El pan **añejo** se pone duro y seco.

Stale bread is dry and hard.

2790   stale bread

un tallo de apio

2791   celery stalk

Un potro es un caballo macho.

2792   stallion

la estampilla, el sello

2793   stamp

pararse, estar de pie

2794   to stand

Las estrellas son rayos de luz vieja.

2795   star

Marisol te **mira fijamente**.

2796   to stare

el estornino

2797   starling

poner en marcha un coche

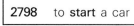

2798   to start a car

estar famélico, morir de hambre

Cuando Marisol dice ''estoy **famélica**'', quiere decir que tiene hambre.
¡No te vas a **morir de hambre**, Marisol!

When Marisol says ''I'm starving'', she means that she is hungry.
You will not starve, Marisol!

2799   to starve

la bencinera, la estación de servicio, **la gasolinera**

2800   gas/petrol* station

la estación de trenes

2801   train/railway* station

la estatua

2802   statue

¡Quédate ahí!

2803   Stay there!

el bistec

2804   steak

robar

2805   to steal

el vapor

2806   steam

Los cuchillos se hacen de **acero**.

2807   Knives are made of **steel**.

empinado

2808   steep

la res, el novillo

2809   steer/bullock*

el tallo

2811   stem

el escalón, el peldaño, la grada

2812   step

¡Me metí en un charco!

2813   to step in

guiar, conducir, dirigir

2810   to steer

Papá preparó **un estofado** para la comida.

2815   stew

el palo, la vara

2816   stick

Voy a **salir** un ratito.

2814   to step out

Vicente tiene las manos **pegajosas**.

2817   sticky

duro, tieso

Malandrín el ladrón recibió una **dura** condena. Amanecí con el cuello **tieso**.

Malandrin the thief received a stiff sentence.
I got up with a stiff neck.

2818   stiff

La picadura me **escuece** y me **duele**.

2819   to sting

la picadura de abeja

2820   sting

Los zorrillos **apestan**.

2821   to stink

Revuelve bien antes de tomártelo.	**las medias**	**atizar**	**el estómago**
2822 to stir	2823 stockings	2824 to stoke	2825 stomach
Los picapedreros pican **piedras**.	**el taburete, la banqueta, el piso**	Yo **me agacho** a recoger la pelota.	**el alto, la parada**
2826 stone	2827 stool	2828 to stoop/bend down*	2829 stop
la tienda, el almacén	¿Quién trae a los niños? **¿La cigüeña?**	**la tormenta, la tempestad**	El Supertipo **detuvo** el tren.
2832 store/shop*	2833 stork	2834 storm	2830 He **stops** the train.
La Tía María nos leyó **un cuento**.	**la cocina**	**derecho, recto**	**una escala** técnica
2835 story	2836 stove/cooker*	2837 straight	2831 to stop over
colar	**esforzarse**	un animalejo muy **raro**	¡Quique se acercó mucho y el gorila lo va a **estrangular**!
2838 to strain	2839 to strain	2840 strange	2841 to strangle

el tirante

2842　　strap

la paja, la pajilla

2843　　straw

la frutilla, la fresa

2844　　strawberry

el arroyo

2845　　stream

el banderín, el gallardete

2846　　streamer/pennant*

la calle

2847　　street

el farol

2848　　street light/lamp*

¿Hasta dónde se podrá **estirar**?

2849　　to stretch

la camilla

2850　　stretcher

la huelga

Los obreros están en **huelga** por mejores salarios.

The workers are on strike for more money.

2851　　strike

No es bueno **golpear** a otra persona.

2852　　to strike

la cuerda, el cordel

2853　　string

un género a **rayas**

2854　　stripe

fuerte

2855　　strong

el alumno, el estudiante

2856　　student

estudiar

2857　　to study

un **animalito de juguete**

2858　　a stuffed animal

el tocón

2859　　stump

Yo prefiero **el submarino** amarillo.

2860　　submarine

restar

2861　　to subtract

chupar
2862   to suck

de repente, precipitadamente
De repente se puso a llover.
Gabriela se fue precipitadamente.

Suddenly, it began to rain.
Gabriela left suddenly.

2863   suddenly

Comer mucha **azúcar** no hace bien.
2864   sugar

el terno, el traje
2865   suit

la maleta, la valija
2866   suitcase

¡Qué lindo es **el verano**!
2867   summer

el sol
2868   sun

el domingo
El domingo es el séptimo día de la semana.

Sunday is the seventh day of the week.

2869   Sunday

Un reloj de sol no se atrasa.
2870   sundial

El girasol gira con el sol.
2871   sunflower

la salida del sol
2872   sunrise

la puesta del sol
2873   sunset

¿Me acompañas al **supermercado**?
2874   supermarket

la cena, la comida
2875   supper/dinner*

seguro
Estoy **seguro** de que mañana será un día soleado.
Seguro que Marisol va mañana.

I am sure tomorrow will be a sunny day.
Marisol will go tomorrow for sure.

2876   sure

la superficie lunar
2877   surface

el cirujano
2878   surgeon

el apellido
Mi nombre es Marisol y mi **apellido** es Martínez.

My first name is Marisol and my surname is Martinez.

2879   surname

una fiesta de **sorpresa**
2880   surprise party

rendirse
2881   to surrender

Estos tipos me tienen rodeado.

2882   to surround

los suspensores, los tirantes

2883   suspenders/braces*

tragar

2884   to swallow

el cisne

2885   swan

permutar, trocar, intercambiar

2886   to swap

¡Un enjambre de abejas asesinas!

2887   swarm

sudar, transpirar

2888   to sweat

el suéter, la chompa, la chomba

2889   sweater/sweatshirt*

barrer

2890   to sweep

dulce

2891   sweet

Tuvimos que **virar bruscamente** a causa de ese gato.

2892   to swerve

nadar

2893   to swim

el columpio

2894   swing

columpiarse

2895   to swing

el interruptor

2896   switch

encender, cambiar, apagar

Enciende las luces, por favor.
Si quieres te cambio el asiento y así ves mejor.
Lo mejor es apagar el televisor.

Switch on the light, please.
Shall we switch seats so you can see better?
It is best to switch off the television.

2897   to switch

abalanzarse, abatirse sobre algo

2898   to swoop

la espada

2899   sword

el sicómoro, el sicomoro

2900   sycamore

¿Te gustan los panqueques con **jarabe**?

2901   syrup

la mesa

2902   table

el mantel
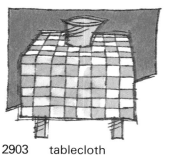

2903   tablecloth

la tableta
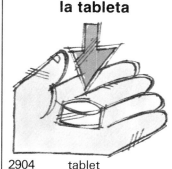

2904   tablet

una tachuela

2905   tack

abordar, atajar

Marisol tendrá que **abordar** pronto el problema.
¿Viste cómo Alfredo **atajó** a Guillermo durante el partido de fútbol?

Marisol must tackle that problem soon.
Did you see how Alfredo tackled Guillermo during the football game?

2906   to tackle

Los renacuajos se convierten en ranas.

2907   tadpole

la cola, el rabo

2908   tail

tomar, coger, asir

2910   to take

desarmar

2911   to take apart

llevar, llevarse

2912   to take away

devolver, llevar de vuelta

2913   to take back

quitarse, sacarse

2914   to take off

despegar

2915   to take off

sacar, extraer

2916   to take out

Compré comida **para llevar**.

2917   take-out/take-away*

el sastre

2909   tailor

el cuento, el chisme, el relato

2918   tale

el talento

Lucía y Marisol demonstraron ser cantantes **de talento**.
Marta tiene mucho **talento** para el teatro.

Lucia and Marisol showed themselves to be talented singers.
Marta has a great talent for acting.

2919   talent

hablar

2920   to talk

alto, espigado

2921 tall

el pandero, la pandereta

2922 tambourine

Los leones circenses son bastante **mansos**.

2923 tame

¡Qué hermoso **bronceado**!

2924 tan

la mandarina

2925 tangerine

enredado, enmarañado

2926 tangled

el tanque, el depósito

2927 tank

el buque tanque, el buque cisterna

2928 tanker

Esta **llave** está goteando.

2929 tap

un rollo de **cinta**

2930 tape

pegar, fijar con cinta adhesiva

2931 to tape

la grabadora, el grabador

2932 tape recorder

la brea, el alquitrán

2933 tar

La flecha dio en **el blanco**.

2934 target

El estragón se usa en las comidas.

2935 tarragon

la tarta, el pastel de frutas

2936 tart

Mi **tarea** es barrer el piso.

2937 task

probar, paladear, saborear, degustar

2938 to taste

sabroso

Esta comida está muy sabrosa.

This is very tasty food.

2939 tasty

el taxi, el coche de alquiler

2940 taxi

una tacita de **té**	La Sra. González nos **enseña** matemáticas.	Ella es **la profesora** de mi curso.	Yo juego en **el equipo** de béisbol.
2941 a cup of **tea**	2942 to **teach**	2943 **teacher**	2944 **team**

la tetera	**la lágrima**	**rasgar, romper, desgarrar**	Nunca **arranques** las páginas de un libro.
2945 **teapot**	2946 **tear**	2947 to **tear**	2948 to **tear out**

el telegrama	**el teléfono**	**llamar por teléfono, telefonear**	**el telescopio**
2949 **telegram**	2950 **telephone**	2951 to **telephone**	2952 **telescope**

La tele es lo mismo que **la televisión**.	**decir, contar, narrar, relatar**	**el genio, el mal humor**	**la temperatura**
		Macabeo tiene mal **genio**. A veces no puede controlar su **mal humor**. *Macabeo has a bad temper. He cannot control his temper.*	
2953 **television**	2954 to **tell**	2955 **temper**	2956 **temperature**

diez manzanitas	raqueta y pelota de **tenis**	una zapatilla de **tenis**	Anoche Marisol durmió en una **tienda de campaña**.
2957 **ten** apples	2958 **tennis** racquet and ball	2959 **tennis** shoe	2960 **tent**

décimo

2961   tenth

un terminal
de computación

2962   terminal

probar el agua

2963   to **test** the water

**agradecer,
dar las gracias**

2964   to **thank**

Al llegar la primavera el
suelo **se deshiela**.

2965   to **thaw**

el teatro

2966   theater / theatre*

allí, ahí, allá

2967   there

el termómetro

2968   thermometer

**tupido, grueso,
denso, espeso**

2969   thick

Ladrón que roba
a **ladrón** . . .

2970   thief

el muslo

2971   thigh

el dedal

2972   thimble

ralo, flaco, delgado

2973   thin

la cosa

Una persona no es una
cosa.
Marisol dice **cosas** muy
graciosas.

*A person is not a thing.
Marisol says many funny
things.*

2974   thing

pensar

2975   to **think**

tercero

2976   third

sediento

2977   thirsty

un cardo burrero

2978   thistle

Las espinas pinchan.

2979   thorn

el hilo

2980   thread

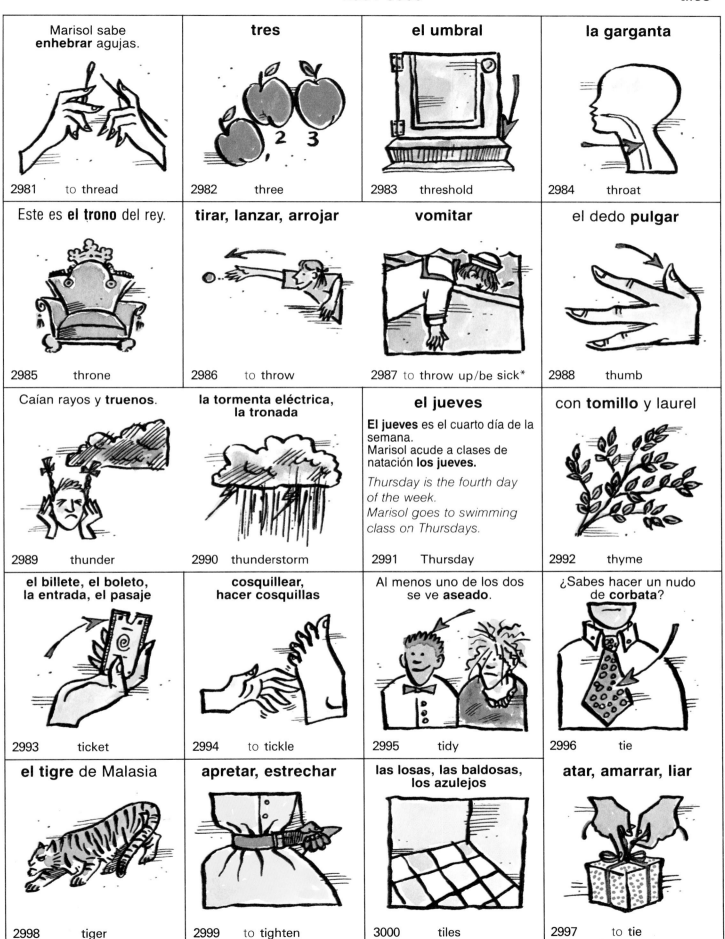

Marisol sabe **enhebrar** agujas.

2981   to thread

tres

2982   three

el umbral

2983   threshold

la garganta

2984   throat

Este es **el trono** del rey.

2985   throne

tirar, lanzar, arrojar

2986   to throw

vomitar

2987   to throw up/be sick*

el dedo **pulgar**

2988   thumb

Caían rayos y **truenos**.

2989   thunder

la tormenta eléctrica, la tronada

2990   thunderstorm

el jueves

El jueves es el cuarto día de la semana.
Marisol acude a clases de natación **los jueves**.

*Thursday is the fourth day of the week.
Marisol goes to swimming class on Thursdays.*

2991   Thursday

con **tomillo** y laurel

2992   thyme

el billete, el boleto, la entrada, el pasaje

2993   ticket

cosquillear, hacer cosquillas

2994   to tickle

Al menos uno de los dos se ve **aseado**.

2995   tidy

¿Sabes hacer un nudo de **corbata**?

2996   tie

el tigre de Malasia

2998   tiger

apretar, estrechar

2999   to tighten

las losas, las baldosas, los azulejos

3000   tiles

atar, amarrar, liar

2997   to tie

¡El bote se está ladeando!

3001   to tilt

¿Qué hora es?

3002   What time is it?

diminuto, menudo

3003   tiny

El bote terminó por volcarse.

3004   to tip

caminar de puntillas

3006   to tiptoe

El coche necesita llantas nuevas.

3007   tire / tyre*

cansado, fatigado

3008   tired

dar propina

3005   to tip

el sapo cancionero

3009   toad

unas tostadas con mantequilla

3010   toast

la tostadora

3011   toaster

hoy día, hoy

Las clases comienzan **hoy día**.
Hoy es el Día de la Madre.
¡Haz tus deberes **hoy** mismo!

School starts today.
Today is Mothers' Day.
Do your homework today!

3012   today

los dedos del pie

3013   toes

Nosotros nos sentamos **juntos**.

3014   We are sitting together.

el inodoro, el retrete, el excusado

3015   toilet

el tomate

3016   tomato

la tumba, la sepultura

3017   tomb

mañana

Mañana será otro día.
Marisol irá **mañana** al museo a ver los dinosaurios.

Tomorrow is another day.
Marisol is going to see dinosaurs at the museum tomorrow.

3018   tomorrow

las tenazas

3019   tongs

Yo no tengo pelos en **la lengua.**

3020   tongue

¡Éste pesa una tonelada!	**las amígdalas**	**las herramientas**	**el diente**
3021 It weighs a **ton**.	3022 tonsils	3023 tools	3024 tooth
el dolor de muelas	**el cepillo de dientes**	**la pasta de dientes**	**la parte superior, la parte de arriba**
3025 toothache	3026 toothbrush	3027 toothpaste	3028 top
Las cajas **se vinieron abajo**.	**la antorcha** olímpica	**el tornado**	**El trompo** gira y gira.
3030 to topple	3031 torch	3032 tornado	3029 top
el torrente, el raudal	**la tortuga**	Martín **arrojó** la pelota a su amiguita.	**tocar**
3033 torrent	3034 tortoise	3035 to toss	3036 to touch
Yo soy un tipo **recio**.	**remolcar**	Marisol tiene **una toalla** favorita.	**la torre** más alta del mundo
3037 I am **tough**.	3038 to tow	3039 towel	3040 tower

Marisol vive en este **pueblo**.	¡Recojan sus **juguetes**, niños!	**calcar**	**el riel, la vía férrea**
3041 town	3042 toys	3043 to trace	3044 track
el tractor	**cambiar, trocar, canjear, permutar**	un embotellamiento de **tráfico**	**el semáforo**
3045 tractor	3046 to trade	3047 traffic	3048 traffic light
el rastro, la pista	**el remolque** para caballitos	¿Te gusta viajar en **tren**?	Macabeo está muy bien **amaestrado**.
3049 trail	3050 trailer	3051 train	3052 to train
el vagabundo	¡No **pisoteen** las flores!	**el trampolín**	Casi todos los vidrios son **transparentes**.
3053 tramp	3054 to trample	3055 trampoline	3056 transparent
transportar, acarrear	**el transportador**	**la trampa** para ratones	Este es Martín, artista del **trapecio**.
3057 to transport	3058 transporter/lorry*	3059 trap	3060 trapeze

Tía Carlina **viaja** con mucha
frecuencia.

3061   to travel

Nos trajeron los tragos
en **bandeja**.

3062   tray

las estrías de
un neumático

3063   tread

el tesoro del filibustero

3064   treasure

el árbol

3065   tree

Yolanda quedó **temblando**
de susto.

3066   to tremble

la zanja, el foso

3067   trench

el juicio, el proceso

3068   trial

Todos **los triángulos**
tienen tres lados.

3069   triangle

truco de magia

3070   trick

El agua **chorrea** despacio.

3071   to trickle

el triciclo

3072   tricycle

Un gatillo no es un gato.

3073   trigger

recortar

3074   to trim

un viaje corto

3075   a short trip

tropezar, dar un traspié

3076   to trip

el trole, el trolebús

3077   trolley bus

A los potrillos les
gusta **trotar**.

3078   to trot

el comedero de animales

3079   trough

los pantalones

3080   trousers

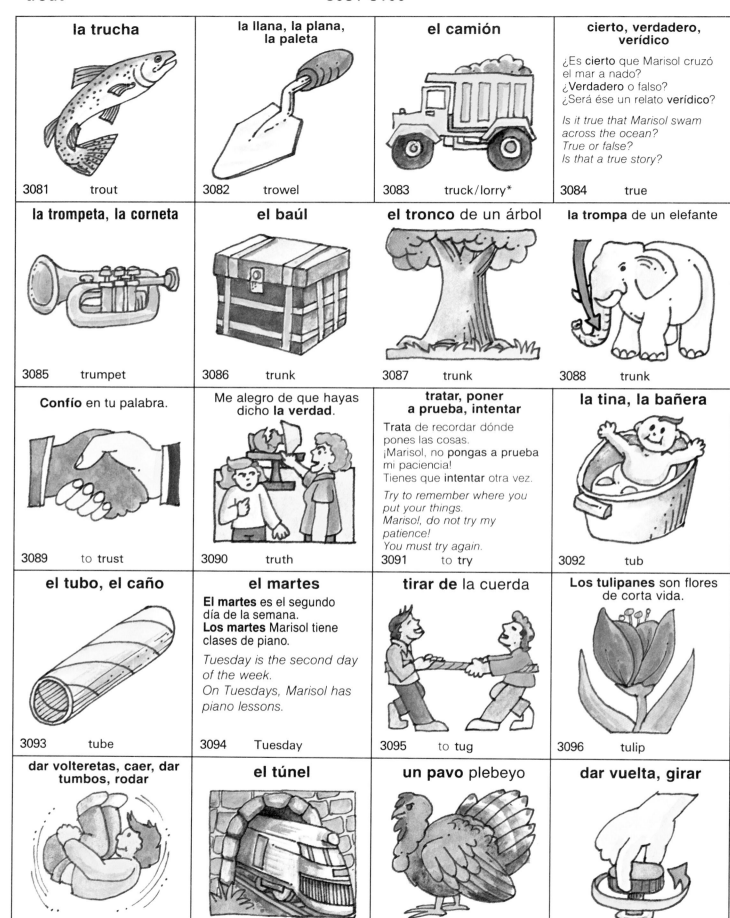

la trucha

3081   trout

la llana, la plana, la paleta

3082   trowel

el camión

3083   truck/lorry*

cierto, verdadero, verídico

¿Es **cierto** que Marisol cruzó el mar a nado?
¿**Verdadero** o falso?
¿Será ése un relato **verídico**?

Is it true that Marisol swam across the ocean?
True or false?
Is that a true story?

3084   true

la trompeta, la corneta

3085   trumpet

el baúl

3086   trunk

el tronco de un árbol

3087   trunk

la trompa de un elefante

3088   trunk

Confío en tu palabra.

3089   to trust

Me alegro de que hayas dicho **la verdad**.

3090   truth

tratar, poner a prueba, intentar

Trata de recordar dónde pones las cosas.
¡Marisol, no **pongas a prueba** mi paciencia!
Tienes que **intentar** otra vez.

Try to remember where you put your things.
Marisol, do not try my patience!
You must try again.

3091   to try

la tina, la bañera

3092   tub

el tubo, el caño

3093   tube

el martes

El martes es el segundo día de la semana.
Los martes Marisol tiene clases de piano.

Tuesday is the second day of the week.
On Tuesdays, Marisol has piano lessons.

3094   Tuesday

tirar de la cuerda

3095   to tug

Los tulipanes son flores de corta vida.

3096   tulip

dar volteretas, caer, dar tumbos, rodar

3097   to tumble

el túnel

3098   tunnel

un pavo plebeyo

3099   turkey

dar vuelta, girar

3100   to turn

apagar

3101   to turn off

encender

3102   to turn on

resultar, salir

Enrique **resultó** ser un mal muchacho.
Las cosas **salieron** bien.

Enrique turned out to be a bad boy.
Things turned out well.

3103   to turn out

Laura le **dio** una **vuelta** a la carne.

3104   to turn over

el nabo

3105   turnip

el plato giratorio

3106   turntable

el color turquesa

3107   turquoise

la torreta, la torrecilla

3108   turret

la tortuga

3109   turtle

Los colmillos son el colmo.

3110   tusk

las pinzas

3111   tweezers

dos veces, el doble

Marisol ha ido al zoológico **dos veces**.
Ricardo tiene **el doble** de libros que yo.

Marisol has been to the zoo twice.
Ricardo has twice as many books as I.

3112   twice

la ramita, la varilla

3113   twig

los gemelos, los mellizos

3114   twins

Las estrellas parpadean en el firmamento.

3115   Stars twinkle.

dar vueltas, hacer girar

3116   to twirl

torcer, retorcer

3117   to twist

dos

3118   two

Papá escribe a máquina todo el santo día.

3119   to type

la máquina de escribir

3120   typewriter

Medusa era **fea** pero tenía un no sé qué . . .

3121 ugly

el paraguas

3122 umbrella

el tío

El hermano de mamá es uno de mis **tíos**.
Mi otro **tío** es el hermano de papá.

My uncle is my mother's brother.
My other uncle is my father's brother.

3123 uncle

bajo, debajo de, menor de

Yo no voy **bajo** ninguna circunstancia.
Marisol se escondió **debajo de** las sábanas.
Los niños **menores de** 5 años no pueden ir.

I am not going under any circumstances.
Marisol is hiding under the covers.
Children under 5 cannot go.

3124 under

entender, comprender

3125 to understand

la ropa interior

3126 underwear

desvestirse, desnudarse

3127 to undress

triste, desconsolada, descontenta

3128 unhappy

Mi **unicornio** azul ayer se me perdió . . .

3129 unicorn

El coronel Buendía usaba **uniforme** de gala.

3130 uniform

la universidad

3131 university

descargar

3132 to unload

abrir la cerradura

3133 to unlock

desenvolver, desempaquetar

3134 to unwrap

derecho, vertical, enhiesto

3135 upright

al revés, patas arriba

3136 upside-down

Mamá **usa** pimienta para cocinar.

3137 to use

Usó tanta que la **gastó** toda.

3138 to use up

Este cortaplumas es muy **útil**.

3139 useful

Para Vigo me voy de **vacaciones**.

3140   vacation/holiday*

el vapor

3141   vapor/vapour*

Ismael **barniza** su escritorio.

3142   to varnish

el jarrón, el florero

3143   vase

un filete de **ternera**

3144   veal

las verduras, las legumbres, las hortalizas

3145   vegetable

Un coche es **un vehículo**.

3146   vehicle

Dulcinea se cubre la cara con **un velo**.

3147   veil

la vena

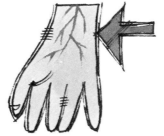

3148   vein

el veneno, la ponzoña

No todas las serpientes tienen **veneno**.
Algunos insectos tienen un veneno llamado **ponzoña**.

Not all snakes have venom.
Some insects have a poison called venom.

3149   venom

La vertical es lo contrario de la horizontal.

3150   vertical

muy, mismo, sumamente

Marisol opina que su hermano es **muy** ingenioso.
Estamos en el centro **mismo** de la ciudad.
Este un libro **sumamente** interesante.

Marisol thinks her brother is very clever.
We are in the very heart of the city.
This is a very interesting book.

3151   very

el chaleco

3152   vest/waistcoat*

Los veterinarios trabajan como animales.

3153   veterinarian/veterinary surgeon*

He aquí **la víctima** del crimen.

3154   victim

un aparato de video

3155   video recorder

Las cintas de video se deben manejar con cuidado.

3156   video tape

la vista

Queremos un cuarto con **vista** al mar.
Todos tenemos nuestro propio punto de **vista**.

We would like a room with a view of the sea.
We each have our own point of view.

3157   view

el pueblo, la aldea

3158   village

el malhechor, el bandido, el villano

3159   villain

Las uvas nacen de **la vid**.

3160   vine

A Marisol le gusta **el vinagre**.

3161   vinegar

Cómpreme usted este ramito de **violetas** . . .

3162   violet

el violín

3163   violin

Para entrar a un país se necesita **una visa**.

3164   visa

visible

Han habido **visibles** cambios en la situación. Invisible es lo contrario de **visible**.

There have been visible changes in the situation. Invisible is the opposite of visible.

3165   visible

Matías fue a **visitar** a su tía al hospital.

3166   to **visit**

la visera

3167   visor

el vocabulario

El que tiene un buen **vocabulario** conoce muchas palabras. Tener un buen **vocabulario** es muy importante. Este diccionario te ayuda a agrandar tu **vocabulario**.

Someone who has a good vocabulary knows many words. A good vocabulary is very important. This dictionary helps increase your vocabulary.

3168   vocabulary

¡Qué buena **voz** tiene!

3169   voice

el volcán

3170   volcano

el vóleibol, la pelota de vóleibol

3171   volleyball

la voluntaria

3172   volunteer

vomitar

3173   to **vomit**

votar

3174   to **vote**

el votante

3175   voter

la vocal

Las vocales del alfabeto son la a, e, i, o y u.

A, E, I, O, U and Y are the only vowels in the alphabet.

3176   vowel

una larga **travesía** por mar.

3177   voyage

Los buitres comen carroña.

3178   vulture

W

Manuel se metió **chapoteando** al agua.	**el wafle, el barquillo**	**la carreta, el carro, el carretón**
3179 to wade	3180 waffle	3181 wagon/cart*
chillar, aullar, llorar, lamentarse	**una cintura** de avispa	Antonia **aguarda** el autobús.	¡Siempre me **despiertan** antes de tiempo!
3182 to wail	3183 waist	3184 to wait	3185 to wake
caminar, andar	**la pared, el muro, la muralla**	**la billetera, la cartera**	mucho ruido y pocas **nueces**
3186 to walk	3187 wall	3188 wallet	3189 walnut
la morsa	**la varita** mágica de Merlín	**vagar, errar**	**querer, necesitar**
3190 walrus	3191 wand	3192 to wander	¿Quién **quiere** más cereal? El letrero dice: "Se **necesitan** albañiles". Marisol **quiere** lavar los platos pero no hay agua. *Who wants more cereal? The sign says: "Bricklayers wanted". Marisol wants to do the dishes but there is no water.* 3193 to want
Marisol y sus amigos odian **la guerra**.	**el vestuario, la ropa**	**la bodega, el almacén, el depósito**	**abrigado**
3194 war	3195 wardrobe	3196 warehouse	3197 warm

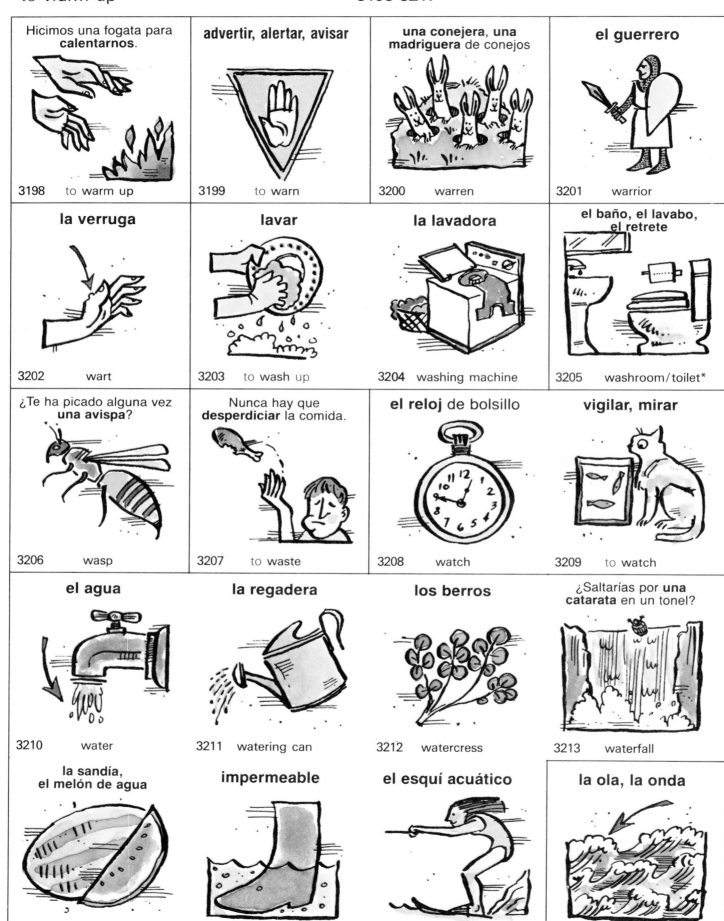

Hicimos una fogata para **calentarnos**.

3198   to warm up

advertir, alertar, avisar

3199   to warn

una conejera, una madriguera de conejos

3200   warren

el guerrero

3201   warrior

la verruga

3202   wart

lavar

3203   to wash up

la lavadora

3204   washing machine

el baño, el lavabo, el retrete

3205   washroom/toilet*

¿Te ha picado alguna vez **una avispa**?

3206   wasp

Nunca hay que **desperdiciar** la comida.

3207   to waste

el reloj de bolsillo

3208   watch

vigilar, mirar

3209   to watch

el agua

3210   water

la regadera

3211   watering can

los berros

3212   watercress

¿Saltarías por **una catarata** en un tonel?

3213   waterfall

la sandía, el melón de agua

3214   watermelon

impermeable

3215   waterproof

el esquí acuático

3216   waterskiing

la ola, la onda

3217   wave

Verónica les **hace señas** a sus amigos.

3218   to wave

Ella tiene el cabello **ondulado**.

3219   wavy

Las velas están hechas de **cera**.

3220   wax

débil, enclenque

3221   weak

Las armas son muy peligrosas.

3222   weapon

llevar, ponerse, vestir, traer puesto

3223   to wear

la comadreja

3224   weasel

¿Cómo está **el tiempo** afuera?

3225   weather

tejer, trenzar, urdir, tramar, entrelazar

3226   to weave

Los patos tienen patas **palmeadas**.

3227   web foot

la boda, el casamiento, el matrimonio

3228   wedding

la cuña

3229   wedge

el miércoles

El **miércoles** es el tercer día de la semana.
Marisol saca la basura **los miércoles.**

Wednesday is the third day of the week.
On Wednesdays, Marisol takes out the garbage.

3230   Wednesday

Los mejores jardines tienen **malezas**.

3231   weed

La semana tiene siete días.

3232   week

el fin de semana

Tía Mercedes viene de visita este **fin de semana**.
El **fin de semana** es el sábado y el domingo.
El hombre del tiempo dijo que llovería este **fin de semana**.

Aunt Mercedes will visit us this weekend.
Saturday and Sunday make a weekend.
The weatherman says it will rain this weekend.

3233   weekend

La gente **llora** cuando está triste.

3234   to weep

pesar

3235   to weigh

un tipo **extraño**

3236   weird

Dolores le **dio la bienvenida** a su amiga.

3237   to welcome

el pozo de agua

3238   well

¡Me siento muy bien!

3239   I feel well.

Cuando el norte está arriba, el oeste queda a la izquierda.

3240   west

mojado, empapado

3241   wet

¡No hay que dejar que las ballenas se extingan!

3243   whale

el muelle, el malecón, el embarcadero

3244   wharf

qué, lo que

¿**Qué** le pasó al pobre Micifuz?
Marisol, ¿**qué** le has hecho a tu gato?
Marisol, ¿escuchas **lo que** te digo?

What happened to poor Micifuz?
Marisol, what did you do to your cat?
Marisol, did you hear what I said?

3245   what

mojar, empapar

3242   to wet

el trigo

3246   wheat

la rueda

3247   wheel

la carretilla

3248   wheelbarrow

la silla de ruedas

3249   wheelchair

cuándo, cuando

¿**Cuándo** vendrá tía Mercedes, papá?
Cuando llegue el fin de semana.
¿Y **cuándo** será eso?

When is Aunt Mercedes coming, Dad?
When the weekend starts.
When is that?

3250   when

dónde, donde, adónde

Nos perdimos y mamá no tiene idea en **dónde** estamos.
Este es el lugar **donde** yo nací.
¿**Adónde** vamos?

We are lost and Mom has no idea where we are.
This is the place where I was born.
Where are we going?

3251   where

¿Cuál de los tres?

3252   which one

gimotear, quejarse

3253   to whine

el látigo

3254   whip

un ave llamada chotacabras

3255   whippoorwill

el batidor

3256   whisk

Micifuz tiene unos largos bigotes.

3257   whisker

Marisol le **susurró** un secreto a su amiga.

3258   to whisper

el pito, el silbato

3259   whistle

silbar, chiflar

3260   to whistle

el color **blanco**

3261   white

¿Quién de ustedes viene?

3262   Who is going?

por qué, cómo es que

Lo que yo quiero saber es **por qué** Marisol tomó mi corbata.
¿**Cómo es que** ella no se acuerda?

I want to know why Marisol took my tie.
Why can she not remember?

3263   why

Las lámparas antiguas tenían **mecha**.

3264   wick

un tipo **malvado**

3265   wicked

ancha, amplia

3266   wide

la esposa, la mujer, la señora

3267   wife

El león es un animal **salvaje**.

3268   The lion is a wild animal.

el sauce llorón

3269   willow

Las flores **se marchitan** si no las riegan.

3270   to wilt

taimado, ladino, astuto

3271   wily

ganar

3272   to win

respingar, recular, encogerse

3273   to wince

el viento

3274   wind

dar cuerda

3275   to wind

una chaqueta **cortaviento**

3276   windbreaker

¡No son gigantes, mi señor, son **molinos de viento**!

3277   windmill

la ventana

3278   window

el parabrisas

3279   windshield/windscreen*

El vino es para que lo beban los grandes.

3280   wine

el ala

3281   wing

El búho sabio te **guiña** un ojo.

3282   to wink

el invierno

3283   winter

limpiar, frotar

3284   to wipe

Este es **un alambre** eléctrico.

3285   wire

sabio, prudente

Mi abuelo es un hombre sabio.
¿Tú crees que sea **prudente** que Marisol camine sola por el bosque?

Grandfather is a wise old man. Do you think that it is wise for Marisol to walk in the forest alone?

3286   wise

pedir **un deseo**

3287   to make a wish

la bruja

3288   witch

el mago, el brujo, el hechicero

3289   wizard

¡Que viene **el lobo**!

3290   wolf

un hombre y **una mujer**

3291   woman

tener curiosidad, querer saber, preguntarse

3292   to wonder

maravilloso

3293   wonderful

la leña, la madera

3294   wood

Los pájaros carpinteros se alimentan de insectos.

3295   woodpecker

el bosque

3296   woods

el tallado en madera, la carpintería

3297   woodwork

Este es un ovillo de **lana**.

3298　wool

¡Pero qué **palabra** más rara!

GLÜRP

3299　word

En la vida nada se hace sin **trabajo**.

3300　work

trabajar, laborar

3301　to work

el taller

3303　workshop

El mundo, ni más ni menos.

3304　world

el gusano, la lombriz

3305　worm

hacer ejercicio

3302　to work out

Mamá **se preocupa** mucho por Marisol.

3306　to worry

la herida, la lesión

3307　wound

envolver

3308　to wrap

la corona de flores

3309　wreath

el naufragio

3310　wreck

el reyezuelo

3311　wren

luchar

3312　to wrestle

estrujar, retorcer, exprimir

3313　to wring

Con esta **muñeca** no se juega.

3314　wrist

el reloj de pulsera

3315　wristwatch

escribir

3316　to write

equivocado, malo, incorrecto

Yo creo que este autobús va en dirección **equivocada**.
Yo sé distinguir entre lo bueno y lo **malo**.
Esta dirección es **incorrecta**.

I think our bus is going the wrong way.
I know the difference between right and wrong.
This is the wrong address.

3317　wrong

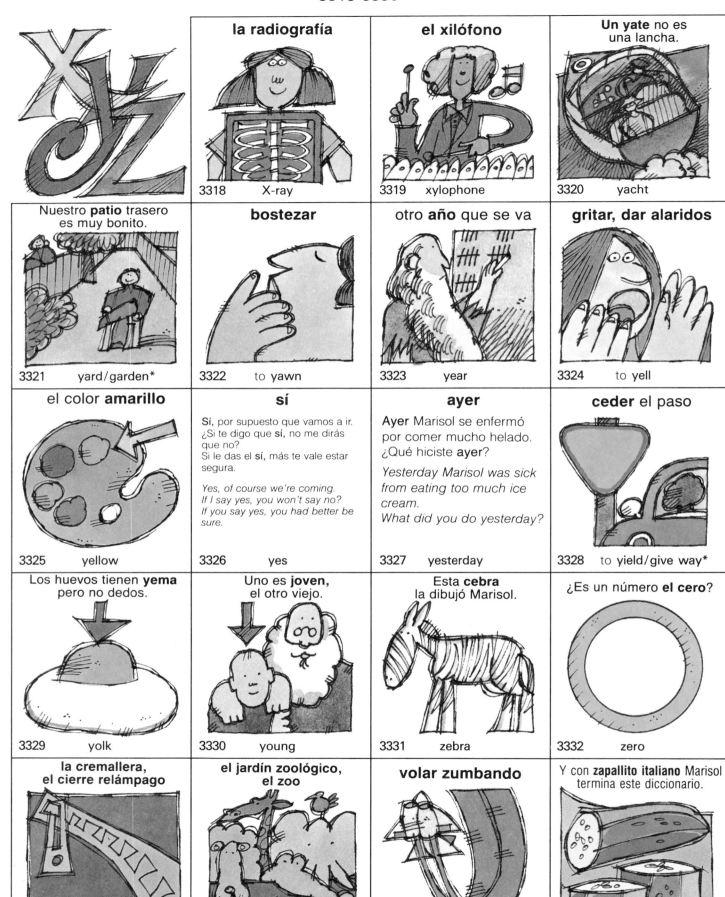

	la radiografía	**el xilófono**	**Un yate** no es una lancha.
	3318 X-ray	3319 xylophone	3320 yacht

Nuestro **patio** trasero es muy bonito.

3321   yard/garden*

bostezar

3322   to yawn

otro **año** que se va

3323   year

gritar, dar alaridos

3324   to yell

el color **amarillo**

3325   yellow

sí

Sí, por supuesto que vamos a ir.
¿Si te digo que **sí**, no me dirás que no?
Si le das el **sí**, más te vale estar segura.

Yes, of course we're coming.
If I say yes, you won't say no?
If you say yes, you had better be sure.

3326   yes

ayer

Ayer Marisol se enfermó por comer mucho helado.
¿Qué hiciste **ayer**?

Yesterday Marisol was sick from eating too much ice cream.
What did you do yesterday?

3327   yesterday

ceder el paso

3328   to yield/give way*

Los huevos tienen **yema** pero no dedos.

3329   yolk

Uno es **joven**, el otro viejo.

3330   young

Esta **cebra** la dibujó Marisol.

3331   zebra

¿Es un número **el cero**?

3332   zero

la cremallera, el cierre relámpago

3333   zipper/zip*

el jardín zoológico, el zoo

3334   zoo

volar zumbando

3335   to zoom

Y con **zapallito italiano** Marisol termina este diccionario.

3336   zucchini/courgette*

a

a 1455
ábaco (el) 1
abadejo (el) 1235
abalanzarse 2216, 2898
abandonar 839
abarrotes (los) 1210
abatirse 2898
abeja (la) 216
abejera (la) 80
abeto (el) 996, 2777
abierto 1952
abofetear 2674
abollar 747
abordar 2906
abrazar 890
abrazarse 890
abrelatas (el) 418
abridor (el) 317
abrigado 3197
abrigo (el) 566, 1976
abril 88
abrir 1953
abrir la cerradura 3133
abrochar 960
abrocharse 960
abuela (la) 1182
abuelo (el) 1181
aburrir 311
acabar de 1510
acampar 415
acanaladura (la) 1214
acantilado (el) 543
acaparar 1341
acarrear 1279, 3057
acaso 1753
accidente (el) 7
acebo (el) 1353
acedera (la) 2730
acedía (la) 2138
aceite (el) 1942
aceituna (la) 1945
acelerador (el) 5, 1111
acelerar 2747
acelga (la) 491
acento (el) 6
acerca de 2
acercarse 86
acero (el) 2807

acezar 2013
acicalarse 1213
ácido 2734
ácido (el) 12
acordarse 2368, 2395
acordeón (el) 8
acostarse 1633
acróbata (el, la) 14
actuación (la) 2085
acuario (el) 90
acusar 9
adelante 1058
adelante de 33
además 239
además de 239
adiós 1168
adivinar 1223
adolorido 2729
adónde 3251
adorar 19
adornar 742
adorno (el) 743
adulto (el) 20
advertir 3199
aerodeslizador (el) 1390
aeropuerto (el) 40
a escala 1817
afeitar 2589
aferrarse 1260
afilado 2584
afilador (el) 2585, 2586
afortunado 1700
Africa 25
agacharse 2828
agalla (la) 1139
agarrar 459, 559, 1127,
   1207, 2560
agarrarse 1260
ágil 31
agitar 2579
agosto 126
agotarse 2478
agradable 2158
agradecer 2964
agrio 2734
agua (el) 3210
agua de lavar los platos
   (el) 786
aguacate (el) 133
aguanieve (el) 2696

aguardar 3184
aguijonear 2182
águila (el) 858
aguja (la) 1890, 2759
agujero (el) 1350
ahí 2967
ahogar 522
ahorrar 2508
aire (el) 36
aire libre (el) 1971
aislamiento (el) 1452
aislante (el) 1452
ají (el) 1385
ajo (el) 1107
al 117
al agua 1975
al lado de 238
al poco rato 2727
al revés 3136
ala (el) 3281
alabar 2224
alacena (la) 1409
alambrada de púas (la)
   169
alambre (el) 3285
álamo (el) 2197
alardear 2624
albahaca (la) 187
albañil (el) 344
albaricoque (el) 87
alberca (la) 2193
albergue (el) 1680
alboroto (el) 2328
álbum (el) 43
alcachofa (la) 104
alcalde (el) 1754
alcanzar 460, 2357
alce (el) 1833
aldea (la) 3158
alegre 1149, 1775
alerce (el) 1574
alertar 3199
aleta (la) 990
aletear 1014
alfabeto (el) 54
alfarería (la) 2214
alfombra (la) 446
alga (la) 2553
algodón (el) 636
alhaja (la) 1488

alicate (el) 2161
aliento (el) 341
aligerar 1640
alimentar 972
alimento (el) 1043
allá 2967
allí 2967
almacén (el) 2613, 2832,
   3196
almacenero (el) 1209,
   2614
almanaque (el) 407
almeja (la) 535
almendra (la) 49
almirante (el) 18
almohadón (el) 2119
almorzar 870
almuerzo (el) 1706
alondra (la) 1577, 2670
alquilar 2398
alquitrán (el) 2135, 2933
alrededor de 99
altavoz (el) 1693
altillo (el) 1681
altiplanicie (la) 2152
alto (el) 2829
alto 1328, 2921
altoparlante (el) 378
alumbrar 1426
aluminio (el) 58
alumno (el) 2856
alzar 1636
alzar en vilo 1297
amable 1529
amaestrar 3052
amapola (la) 2198
amargo 258
amarillo 3325
amarrar 250, 2997
ambos 315
ambulancia (la) 60
a menudo 1941
americana (la) 272
amiga (la) 1073
amígdala (la) 3022
amodorrado 840
amontonarse 1395
amor (el) 1695
amoroso 1697
amplio 3266

balancín (el) 2557
balanza (la) 2515
balcón (el) 153
balde (el) 368, 1994
baldosa (la) 3000
baliza (la) 384
ballena (la) 3243
ballet (el) 157
balón (el) 155, 1045
balsa (la) 2333
banana (la) 160
banco (el) 166, 234
bandada (la) 1027
bandeja (la) 3062
bandera (la) 1011
banderín (el) 2846
bandido (el) 3159
bañera (la) 194, 3092
baño (el) 192, 193, 3205
banqueta (la) 2827
bar (el) 168
barajar 2631
baranda (la) 165, 1256, 2335
barato 497
baraúnda (la) 2328
barba (la) 206
barbilla (la) 515
barcaza (la) 173
barnizar 3142
barquillo (el) 608, 3180
barra (la) 167
barra de labios (la) 1660
barranco (el) 2353
barrer 2890
barrera (la) 182
barril (el) 179
barrilete (el) 1537
barro (el) 1854
base (la) 183, 184
basta 900
bastilla (la) 1310
bastón (el) 424
bastón de hockey (el) 1346
basura (la) 1103, 2466
basural (el) 850
basurero (el) 850
bate (el) 190
batidor (el) 3256

batidora (la) 1813
batir 164
batir palmas 537
baúl (el) 3086
bazar (el) 198
bebé (el) 140
beber 829
becerro (el) 408
beige 227
béisbol (el) 185
bellota (la) 13
bencina (la) 1110
bencinera (la) 2800
berenjena (la) 877
berro (el) 3212
besar 1534
besarse 1534
beso (el) 1535
bestia (la) 207
betarraga (la) 220
biblioteca (la) 1628
bicho (el) 372, 666
bici (la) 246
bicicleta (la) 244, 714
bien 992, 2263, 2422, 3239
bien educado 2188
bien parecido 1257
bigote (el) 1847, 3257
billar (el) 249
billete (el) 247, 2993
billetera (la) 3188
binoculares (los) 251
bisagra (la) 1334
bisonte (el) 371
bistec (el) 2804
bizcocho (el) 255
blanco (el) 2934
blanco 3261
blanqueador (el) 273
bloc (el) 1988
blusa (la) 288
bobina de hilo (la) 2765
boca (la) 1848
bocina (la) 1374
boda (la) 3228
bodega (la) 471, 3196
boina (la) 237
bol (el) 324
boleto (el) 2993

bolígrafo (el) 2074
bolita (la) 1732
bolsa (la) 147, 2215
bolsillo (el) 2173
bolso (el) 2294
bomba (la) 998, 2281
bomba de gasolina (la) 1112
bombear 2282
bombero (el) 1001
bombilla (la) 1639
bondadoso 1120
bonito 2234
bordado (el) 891
borde (el) 874
borde de la acera (el) 698
borrego (el) 1561
bosque (el) 1051, 3296
bostezar 3322
bota (la) 308
botar 851, 1132
bote (el) 298, 417
bote de goma (el) 770
bote salvavidas (el) 1635
botella (la) 316
botica (la) 2097
boticario (el) 2096
botón (el) 370, 397
botones (el) 2205
boxeador (el) 326
boya (la) 384
bozal (el) 1867
brazalete (el) 329
brazo (el) 95
brea (la) 2135, 2933
brécol (el) 354
bribón (el) 674
brida (la) 348
brillante 350, 2603
brillar 2600
brincar 1368
brocha (la) 364, 1999
broche (el) 355
brócoli (el) 354
broma (la) 1495
bronceado (el) 2924
brote (el) 370
bruja (la) 3288
brujo (el) 2728, 3289

brújula (la) 597
bruma (la) 1284
bruñir 2187
brusco 293
budín (el) 2273
bueno 1167, 1907
buey (el) 1983
búfalo (el) 371
bufanda (la) 2521
buhardilla (la) 1681
búho (el) 1981
buitre (el) 3178
buldozer (el) 376
bumerang (el) 307
buque cisterna (el) 2928
buque tanque (el) 2928
burbuja (la) 367
burlarse 1815
burro (el) 803
bus (el) 389, 561
buscar 2548

C

cabalgar 2419
caballería (la) 465
caballero (el) 1121
caballete (el) 865
caballito (el) 2192
caballito de mar (el) 2543
caballo (el) 1378
cabaña (la) 400, 635
cabecera (la) 1289
cabellera (la) 1237
cabestrillo (el) 2686
cabeza (la) 1287
cable (el) 402
cable de cierre (el) 1505
cable de puente (el) 1505
cabo (el) 431
cabra (la) 1162
cabrito (el) 1520
cacahuete (el) 2060
cacao (el) 568
cacharro (el) 2214
cachorro (el) 2290

cacto (el) 403
cactus (el) 403
cada 914
cada uno 857
cadáver (el) 631
cadena (la) 480
cadera (la) 1336
caer 946, 947, 3097
caerse 836, 946
caerse al suelo 947
caerse de 948
café (el) 571
café 360
caimán (el) 48
caja (la) 325, 453, 660
caja de cartón (la) 451
caja fuerte (la) 2487
cajón (el) 818
calabacín (el) 2779
calabaza (la) 2283, 2779
calabozo (el) 853
calamar (el) 2782
calandria (la) 2670
calato 1872
calavera (la) 2668
calcar 3043
calcetín (el) 2717
calculador (el) 406
calculadora (la) 406
caldera (la) 463, 1092
calefactor (el) 1296
caleidoscopio (el) 1511
calendario (el) 407
caléndula (la) 1736
calentar 1295
calentarse 3198
calidad (la) 2306
callado 2641
calle (la) 2847
callejón (el) 47
calmada 412
caluroso 1383
calvo 154
cama (la) 213
cámara (la) 414
camarón (el) 2628
cambiar 2401, 2897, 3046
cambiarse 486
cambio (el) 485
camello (el) 413

camilla (la) 2850
caminar 3186
caminar de puntillas
 3006
camino (el) 2437
camión (el) 3083
camión de bomberos
 (el) 998
camión de volteo (el)
 852
camión tolva (el) 852
camisa (la) 2606
campamento (el) 416
campana (la) 229
campeón (el) 484
campo (el) 642, 982
caña (la) 2378, 2446
canal (el) 419, 487
canalete (el) 1990
canario (el) 420
canasta (la) 188
cancelar 410
cancha de tenis (la) 646
canción (la) 2726
canción de cuna (la) 1703
candado (el) 1992
canguro (el) 1512
canica (la) 1732
canilla (la) 2599
canjear 3046
caño (el) 3093
canoa (la) 427
cañón (el) 180, 425, 429
cansado 3008
cantar 2646
cantera (la) 2309
cantidad (la) 2307
canto (el) 2726
capa (la) 432, 1595
capitán (el) 434, 2666
capítulo (el) 488
capó (el) 1364
capturar 435
capucha (la) 1363
capullo (el) 370
cara (la) 937
caracol (el) 2706
carácter (el) 489
carámbano (el) 1416
caramelo (el) 423

caravana (la) 437
carbón (el) 490, 563
carcaj (el) 2321
cárcel (la) 1476
cardo (el) 2978
carencia (la) 1888
carga (la) 442
cargador (el) 2205
cargar 492, 1671, 1672
carnaval (el) 444
carne (la) 1025, 1762
carnicero (el) 394
caro 925
carpintero (el) 445
carpintería (la) 3297
carreta (la) 450, 3181
carrete (el) 2381
carrete de hilo (el) 2765
carretera (la) 1331, 2437
carretilla (la) 3248
carretón (el) 450, 3181
carrito (el) 447
carro (el) 436, 3181
carrobomba (el) 998
carta (la) 438, 1623,
 1772, 2156
cartel (el) 248, 2211, 2638
cartera (la) 349, 2294,
 3188
cartero (el) 1718
cartón (el) 439
casa (la) 1355, 1389, 2137
casamiento (el) 3228
casarse 1740
cascabel (el, la) 2349,
 2350
cascanueces (el) 1925
cáscara (la) 2424
casco (el) 1307, 1365,
 1397
casero (el) 1569
casi 50
casis (el) 263
castaña (la) 505
castaña de cajú (la) 455
castigar 2287
castigo (el) 2288
castillo (el) 456
castor (el) 210
catálogo (el) 458

catarata (la) 3213
caucho (el) 2465
cavar 766
cazar 1402
cebada (la) 176
cebo (el) 148
cebolla (la) 1950
cebolleta (la) 519
cebollín (el) 519
cebra (la) 3331
ceder 3328
ceja (la) 359, 933
celebrar 468
cellisca (la) 2681
célula (la) 470
cemento (el) 472
cena (la) 772, 2875
cenar 871
cenicero (el) 108
ceniza (la) 107
centeno (el) 2482
centímetro (el) 474
centinela (el) 2567
centro (el) 473
cepillar 362
cepillarse 362
cepillo (el) 363
cepillo de carpintero (el)
 2142
cepillo de dientes (el)
 365, 3026
cepillo para el pelo (el)
 1238
cera (la) 3220
cerca (la) 975
cerca 1881
cerca de 99
cerda (la) 2736
cerdo (el) 2113
cereal (el) 477
cerebro (el) 331
cereza (la) 503
cero 3332
cerradura (la) 1677
cerrar 548
cerrar con pestillo 1581
cerrar de un portazo
 2672
cerrar el paso 282
cerro (el) 2420

meter un gol 2532
meterse 1129
meterse en 2813
método (el) 1783
metro (el) 1782
metrónomo (el) 1784
mezclar 1812
micrófono (el) 1785
microonda (la) 1787
microscopio (el) 1786
miel (la) 1358
miembro (el) 1771
miércoles (el) 3230
migaja (la) 685
milagro (el) 1803
milla (la) 1792
mina (la) 1796
mineral (el) 1798
minero (el) 1797
minuta (la) 1772
minuto (el) 1802
mirar 1686, 3209
mirar fijamente 2796
mirlo (el) 261
misil (el) 1808
mismo 2497, 3151
misterio (el) 2418
mitad (la) 1241
mitón (el) 1811
modales (los) 1728
moderno 1818
moho (el) 1838
mojado 1819, 3241
mojar 3242
molde (el) 1842, 2049
moler 1206, 1742
molino (el) 1794
molino de viento (el)
    3277
momento (el) 1822
moneda (la) 574
mono (el) 1504, 1825
mono 712
monopatín (el) 2658
monstruo (el) 1827
montaña (la) 1845
montar 1844, 2419
montar guardia 1222
montarse 1844
montículo (el) 1843

montón (el) 1292, 2116
montura (la) 2486
monumento (el) 1829
mora (la) 260
morado (el) 2292
morder 256
mordisco (el) 257
mordisquear 1906
morir 763
morir de hambre 2799
morirse 763
morsa (la) 3190
mortal 962
mortero (el) 1835
mosaico (el) 1836
mosca (la) 1036
mosquito (el) 1837
mostacho (el) 1847
mostaza (la) 1866
mostrador (el) 641
mostrar 2623
moto (la) 1841
motocicleta (la) 1841
motín (el) 2429
motoneta (la) 2530
motor (el) 896, 1840
motor a chorro (el) 1485
motor a reacción (el)
    1485
motosierra (la) 481
mover hacia adelante 21
moverse 1849
movimiento (el) 1850
mozo de cuadra (el)
    1212, 2205
mucho 1853
muchos 1729
mueble (el) 1093
muelle (el) 797, 2112,
    2772, 3244
muérdago (el) 1810
muerto 736
mugre (la) 775
mugriento 1204, 2691
mujer (la) 3267, 3291
mujer policía (la) 2186
mula (la) 1855
muleta (la) 688
mulo (el) 1855
multa (la) 991

multiplicar 1856
mundo (el) 3304
muñeca (la) 800, 3314
muralla (la) 3187
murciélago (el) 191
muro (el) 3187
músculo (el) 1859
museo (el) 1860
musgo (el) 1838
música (la) 1862
músico (el) 1863
muslo (el) 2971
muy 3151

n

nabo (el) 3105
nacer 312
nacimiento (el) 253
nación (la) 1876
nada 75
nadar 2983
nadie 1919
nailon (el) 1926
naipe (el) 438, 2156
naranja (el) 1959
naranja (la) 1958
narciso (el) 718
nariz (la) 1923
narrar 2954
natural 1877
naturaleza (la) 1878
naufragio (el) 2605,
    3310
navaja de afeitar (la)
    2356
nave (la) 2604
nave espacial (la) 2738
navegar 1880
neblina (la) 1040
necesario 1883
necesitar 1889, 3193
necio 2643
néctar (el) 1886
negro 259
nene (el) 140
neón (el) 1895
nervio (el) 1897

nervioso 1898
nevera (la) 1072
nido (el) 1899
niebla (la) 1809
nieta (la) 1180
nieto (el) 1180
nieve (la) 2712
nilón (el) 1926
niña (la) 511, 1144
ninguna parte 77
ninguno de los dos 1894
niño (el) 327
niño explorador (el)
    2533
níquel (el) 1908
nivelado 1625
niveladora (la) 376
no 1916
no estar 135
no gustar 787
noble (el) 1918
noble 1917
noche (la) 1911
nombre (el) 1873
norte (el) 1922
nota (la) 1738
noticia (la) 1903
novedad (la) 1903
noveno 1915
novia (la) 345
novillo (el) 2809
novio (el) 346, 1211
nube (la) 553
nudillo (el) 1548
nudo (el) 1546
nueva (la) 1903
nueve 1914
nuevo 1902
nuez (la) 1924, 3189
nuez de acajú (la) 455
nunca 1901
nutria (la) 1969

o

o 1957
oasis (el) 1929
oblongo 1930

recortar 711, 546, 3074
recostarse 1633
rectángulo (el) 2376
recto 2837
recular 3273
recuperarse 2375
redondo 2461
reflector (el) 2549
reflejo (el) 2383
refrigerador (el) 1072, 2384
regadera (la) 3211
regalo (el) 1136, 2230
regazo (el) 1573
región (la) 2386
regla (la) 2472
regordete 2168
rehusar 2385
reina (la) 2312
reina mora (la) 1371
reír 1584
reírse 1584
reírse tontamente 1138
reja (la) 975
rejilla (la) 2538
relatar 2954
relato (el) 2918
relinchar 1892
rellano (el) 1568
reloj (el) 547, 3208
reloj de arena (el) 1388
reloj de pulsera (el) 3315
reloj de sol (el) 2870
relumbrar 2743
remar 1991, 2463
remedio (el) 1765
remiendo (el) 2045
remitir 2564
remo (el) 1928
remolacha (la) 220
remolcar 3038
remolque (el) 3050
remoto 2396
renacuajo (el) 2907
rendirse 1147, 2881
reñir 2308
reno (el) 2390
reparar 2399
repartir 746, 1251
repetir 2400

repique (el) 2059
repisa (la) 2594
repisa para libros (la) 306
repollito de Bruselas (el) 366
repollo (el) 399
reponer 2401
reposacabeza (el) 1289
reposar 2393
represa (la) 723
reprobar 939
reptil (el) 2403
repuesto (el) 2741
repugnante 1215
res (la) 2809
resbalar 2688
resbalarse 2663, 2688
resbalín (el) 2683
resbaloso 2690
rescatar 2404
reservado 2249
resguardo (el) 2596
resolver 2723
resoplar 2275
resorte (el) 2772
respingar 3273
respirar 342
resplandeciente 2603
responder 2402
responsable 2406
respuesta (la) 70
restar 2861
restaurante (el) 2408
restorán (el) 2408
resultar 3103
retorcer 3117, 3313
retrasado 1582
retrato (el) 2206
retrete (el) 3015, 3205
retroceder 143
retrovisor (el) 2364
retumbo (el) 2474
reunión (la) 1768
reventar 387, 2196
reventarse 387
revisar 499
revista (la) 1709
revoltoso 1879
revolver 2822

rey (el) 1530
reyezuelo (el) 3311
rezar 2226
riachuelo (el) 667
rico 2417
riel (el) 3044
rienda (la) 2391
riesgo (el) 2434
rima (la) 2413
rincón (el) 630
rinoceronte (el) 2411
riñón (el) 1522
río (el) 2436
ripio (el) 1192
rival (el) 2435
rizado 701
rizo de agua (el) 2432
robar 2805
roble (el) 1927
roca (la) 319, 2442
rociar 2770
rocío (el) 756
rodada (la) 2481
rodar 2448, 3097
rodear 2882
rodilla (la) 1540
rodillo (el) 2450
rojo 2377
roldana (la) 2278
rollizo 2168
rollo (el) 2447
romero (el) 2457
romo 293
rompecabezas (el) 1489, 2301
romper 337, 2947
romperse 2708
ronco 1342
ronronear 2293
ropa (la) 551, 3195
ropa blanca (la) 1653
ropa de cama (la) 1653
ropa interior (la) 3126
ropa sucia (la) 1588
ropero (el) 549
rosa (la) 2456
rosado (el) 2127
rosado 2458
rostro (el) 937
rubí (el) 2467

rubio 283
ruborizarse 294
rueda (la) 3247
ruedo (el) 1310
rugir 2438
ruibarbo (el) 2412
ruido (el) 1920
ruina (la) 2471
ruiseñor (el) 1912
rumbo (el) 774

S

sábado (el) 2505
sábana (la) 2593
sabandija (la) 372
sabanero (el) 1757
saber (el) 2525
saber 1547
sabio 3286
sabor (el) 1021
saborear 898, 2938
sabroso 2939
sacacorchos (el) 628
sacapuntas (el) 2587
sacar 2397, 2916
sacar con cuchara o pala 2529
sacarse 2914
saco (el) 2483
saco de dormir (el) 2679
sacudir 2579
sagrado 1354, 2484
sal (la) 2495
sala (la) 1669, 2452
sala de baño (la) 193
sala de clases (la) 538
sala de estar (la) 1669
salchicha (la) 2507
salida del sol (la) 2872
salir 922, 2433, 2814, 3103
salir a chorros 2784
salirse 839
salmón (el) 2494
salón (el) 1669
salpicar 2761
salsa (la) 2506

saltador 1503
saltamontes (el) 1189
saltar 1500, 2196, 2665
saltar a 1501, 1502
saludar 1201, 2496
salvaje 3268
sanar 699, 1290
sandalia (la) 2499
sandía (la) 3214
sandwich (el) 2500
sangrar 274
sangre (la) 284
sapo (el) 3009
saquito (el) 2215
sarampión (el) 1760
sardina (la) 2502
sarpullido (el) 2346
sartén (la) 1082
sastre (el) 2909
satélite (el) 2503
sauce (el) 3269
savia (la) 2501
se prohibe 2255
secador (el) 1240
secadora (la) 845
secar 843
seco 842
secreto (el) 2555
secuestrar 1332, 1521
sediento 2977
seguir 1042
segundo 2554
seguro 478, 2876
seis 2654
seleccionar 2732
sello (el) 2793
selva (la) 1507
semáforo (el) 3048
semana (la) 3232
sembrar 2737
semicírculo (el) 2563
semilla (la) 2558
señalar 2639
sencillo (el) 485
sencillo 2645
sendero (el) 2046
señora (la) 1556, 3267
sensato 2698
sensible 2565
sentarse 2653

sentencia (la) 2566
sentir 973
sentir lástima 2136
sentirse 973
separado 78
separar 2732
septiembre 2568
séptimo 2571
sepultar 388
sepultura (la) 1191, 3017
ser 199
ser dueño de 1982
serpentín (el) 573
serpiente (la) 2707
serrar 2510
serrucho (el) 2509
servilleta (la) 1874
servir 2569
seto (el) 1300
sexto 2655
shorts (los) 2618
si 1422
sí 3326
sicómoro (el) 2900
sicomoro (el) 2900
siempre 59
siempre verde (el) 913
sierra de cadena (la) 481
siete 2570
siglo (el) 476
signo de exclamación
   (el) 918
siguiente 1905
silbar 3260
silbato (el) 3259
silencioso 2641
silla (la) 482
silla de ruedas (la) 3249
sillón (el) 96, 637
simio (el) 79
simple 2645
sin adorno 2139
sin remedio 1370
singular 2647
sino 393
sinsonte (el) 1816
sirena (la) 1774, 2651
snorkel (el) 2711
sobaco (el) 98
sobre (el) 903

sobrecubierta (la) 1474
sobrenombre (el) 1909
sobretodo (el) 1976
sobrina (la) 1910
sobrino (el) 1896
sofá (el) 637, 2719
soga (la) 2455
sol (el) 2868
soldado (el) 2721
solitario 1684
solo 51
sólo 1510
soltar 1621, 2394
soltarse 588
sombra (la) 2577
sombrero (el) 1276
sonajero (el) 2349
soñar 820
sonreír 1205
sopa (la) 2733
soplar 290
sorber 2650
sordo 737
sorpresa (la) 2880
sostén (el) 328
sostener 1348, 2261
sótano (el) 186, 471
suave 2704, 2720
sube y baja (el) 2557
subir 1160
subirse 1131
submarino (el) 2860
subterráneo (el) 186
sucio 776
sudar 2888
suelo (el) 1029, 1216
suelto 1689
sueño (el) 819
suéter (el) 2279, 2889
sujetar 1349
sumamente 3151
sumar 16
superficie (la) 2877
supermercado (el) 2874
suplicar 2157
sur (el) 2735
surco (el) 1214
suspender 410
suspensores (los) 2883
suspirar 2637

susurrar 3258

t

tabla a vela (la) 2489
tablero (el) 296, 2010
tablero de instrumentos
   (el) 732
tableta (la) 2904
tablón (el) 2144
taburete (el) 2827
tachar 680
tacho de la basura (el)
   1104
tachuela (la) 2905
taimado 3271
tal como 106
tal vez 1753
taladrar 826
taladro (el) 827
talento (el) 2919
talla (la) 2656
tallado en madera (el)
   3297
taller (el) 3303
tallo (el) 2791, 2811
talón (el) 1302
también 57
tambor (el) 841
tan . . . como 106
tanque (el) 2405, 2927
tapa (la) 649, 1631
tapabarro (el) 976
tapacubos (el) 1393
tapar 648
tapete (el) 446
tapiz (el) 446
tapón (el) 2165
tarde (la) 27
tarea (la) 1356, 2937
tarjar 680
tarro (el) 417
tarro de la basura (el)
   1104
tarta (la) 2936
taxi (el) 2940
taza (la) 696
tazón (el) 324

u